COST-
EFFECTIVENESS

NEW PERSPECTIVES IN EVALUATION

Series Editor: Nick L. Smith

Northwest Regional Educational Laboratory

THE BOOKS IN THIS SERIES reflect an emerging awareness among evaluation practitioners and theorists that evaluation involves *more* than conducting an experimental study in an applied setting. Evaluation is increasingly recognized as a highly complex technical, economic, political, and social activity requiring the skills of many professionals—lawyers, economists, artists, and scientists, in addition to psychologists, sociologists, political scientists, and other applied social research specialists.

The purpose of this series is to deepen methodological discussions of evaluation and to improve evaluation practice. Beginning with Volume 1, this series strives to provide readers with new ways to view the evaluative enterprise and innovative tools compatible with these emerging perspectives. Written by some of the field's most creative theorists and practitioners, these volumes will share the adventure of uncovering new approaches to an exciting young discipline and disseminate useful guidelines for the expansion and improvement of its practice.

BOOKS IN THIS SERIES

Additional titles in preparation

COST - EFFECTIVENESS
A Primer

Henry M. Levin

NEW PERSPECTIVES IN EVALUATION
Volume 4

*This volume published in cooperation with
the Northwest Regional Educational Laboratory*

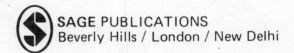
SAGE PUBLICATIONS
Beverly Hills / London / New Delhi

This volume of New Perspectives in Evaluation is published in cooperation with the Northwest Regional Educational Laboratory.

This work was developed under contract #400-80-0105 with the National Institute of Education, Education Department. However, the content does not necessarily reflect the position or policy of that agency and no official endorsement of these materials should be inferred.

For information address:

SAGE Publications, Inc.
275 South Beverly Drive
Beverly Hills, California 90212

SAGE Publications India Pvt. Ltd.
C-236 Defence Colony
New Delhi 110 024, India

SAGE Publications Ltd
28 Banner Street
London EC1Y 8QE, England

Printed in the United States of America

Library of Congress Cataloging in Publication Data

Levin, Henry M.
    Cost-effectivenesss : a primer.

    (New perspectives in evaluation ; v. 4)
    Includes bibliographies.
    1. Cost effectiveness. I. Title. II. Series.
HD47.4.L48   1983   658.4'012   83-17681
ISBN 0-8039-2152-7
ISBN 0-8039-2153-5 (pbk.)

FIRST PRINTING

Contents

Acknowledgments

An earlier draft of this volume was prepared under the aegis of the Research on Evaluation Program of the Northwest Regional Educational Laboratory. I am indebted to Nick Smith of the Northwest Regional Educational Laboratory, Randy Ebert of the Department of Economics at the University of Oregon, and Alex Law of the Department of Education, State of California, for extremely helpful advice and comments. I am especially grateful to Catherine O'Connor, who assisted me in surviving the pressures and pains of producing the final manuscript, to Gail Meister for constructing the index, and to Louis Woo for preparing Table 4.1.

This book is dedicated to David James Levin.

CHAPTER *1*

Introduction to Cost Analysis

OBJECTIVES

1. *Define the objectives of the Primer.*
2. *Define "cost analysis."*
3. *Identify and describe four modes of analysis.*

ALTHOUGH THE TERM "cost-effectiveness" has entered the jargon of politics, administration, and evaluation, there is surprisingly little cost-effectiveness analysis in any area of social endeavor. Politicians refer to cost-effectiveness analysis as a way of making better government decisions. Administrators view it as a method of choosing among competing alternatives in the light of constant or declining budgetary constraints. Evaluators refer to the tool as a way of providing more complete information for decision makers than the usual evaluation that addresses only the results of alternative interventions. As with many fashionable trends, it seems that everyone is talking about it, but no one is doing it. One of the major reasons for the dearth of cost-effectiveness analysis seems to be that few administrators and evaluators have received training in the development and use of the tool. If this premise is correct, it is reasonable to believe that an introduction to cost analysis might encourage and enable such individuals to incorporate this approach into their evaluations and decisions. That is the purpose of this primer, to introduce to the active administrator and evaluator the rationale and methodology of cost analysis.

Cost analysis of social programs includes a number of broad conceptual and operational principles that apply equally well to all areas of public endeavor, including education, health, criminal justice, transportation, and national resources. However, the teaching effectiveness of a primer is likely to be most effective when it is placed within a concrete set of applications. For this reason I have chosen a particular field in which to apply the analysis — the field of education. Education is a particularly amenable topic because it is a subject that is readily familiar to almost everyone, and it is a public activity that has been hit particularly hard by the types of budgetary constraints that require careful planning and evaluation that takes account of costs.

As education faces increasingly the pressures of competition for public dollars, a declining enrollment base, inflation, and ever-increasing demands on the schools for new programs, a way must be found to choose among competing alternatives. Standard evaluation approaches take account only of the effects of alternatives, such as the number of students served, the impact on test scores, and so on. But, cost-effectiveness analysis takes account of both the costs and effects of selecting alternatives, making it possible to choose those alternatives that provide the best results for any given resource outlay or that minimize the resource utilization for any given outcome.

Why should an educational evaluator or administrator be concerned with cost-effectiveness analysis? The most superficial answer to this question is that reference to such analysis is often an important source of persuasion. By saying that one has compared the cost-effectiveness of different approaches and found a particular one to be most cost-effective, one can often disarm opponents. (Unfortunately, this is the principal way in which the terminology is often used in the educational sector.) The rationale for this primer goes beyond such banality. Cost-effectiveness analysis should be a topic of concern because it can lead to a more efficient use of educational resources; it can reduce the costs of reaching particular objectives; and it can expand what can be accomplished for any particular budget or other resource constraint.

Policy decisions in the public sector must be based increasingly upon a demonstrated consideration of both the costs and effects of such decisions. Tax and expenditure limitation movements, declining enrollments, and inflation all have negative impacts on educational budgets, and it is important to take costs into account as well as other aspects of the alternatives. Yet, few evaluators or educational administrators have received training in the nature, development, or use of cost-effectiveness analyses. The standard courses and instructional materials for both evaluators and educational administrators are generally devoid of this subject.

Purpose

The purpose of this primer is to provide a partial resolution for this dilemma for both evaluators and educational administrators through a systematic introduction to the use of cost analysis in educational evaluation. Accordingly, the primer has been written with the intention of familiarizing this audience with the nature and use of cost-analytic tools, as well as showing them how to plan and implement a study in this domain. Cost analysis in educational evaluation refers to the use of a broad set of techniques for evaluation and decision making, including cost-effectiveness, cost-benefit, cost-utility, and cost-feasibility. Each type of analysis will be developed separately for consideration, but I will refer to the group of cost techniques taken together as cost analysis in evaluation.

The audience that the work addresses is not limited only to educational evaluators and administrators, but the primary applications are confined to subjects of interest to this group. It is believed that readers from other areas will easily be able to generalize and apply the techniques and concepts to needs in their domain.

Goals

The specific goals of this primer are the following:

(1) to provide an understanding of what is meant by cost-effectiveness analysis and its variants;

(2) to provide an understanding of the appropriate use of cost-effectiveness analysis in a policy-oriented or decision-oriented framework;

(3) to provide an understanding of basic problems in constructing and implementing a cost-effectiveness analysis in education;

(4) to provide an understanding of the identification of cost factors and their measurement;

(5) to provide an understanding of the identification of effects and benefits and their measurement; and

(6) to provide an understanding of how to use the results of cost-effectiveness studies.

These are primary objectives and should be accomplishable for all serious readers. That is, an educational administrator or evaluator who works his or her way through this primer, doing the various readings and exercises, should be able to accomplish all of these goals.

In addition, it is expected that this primer can serve a different need, which will vary among members of our audience. Some educational administrators and evaluators will wish to go beyond learning about the method and its uses to understanding how to actually apply the method to evaluation and administration within their own work settings. For example, an educational administrator may wish to ascertain how to do studies of cost-effectiveness among various alternatives for providing reading instruction, school lunches, or designing budget cuts. An educational evaluator may wish to learn how to augment a standard evaluation of alternatives with information on costs. While this primer is not designed to train such persons to do these tasks in the absence of other training or assistance, it should be considered a first step in that direction. By mastering this introduction, an evaluator or administrator should be able to work effectively with a technical specialist on cost-effectiveness analysis or should be able to undertake additional study in mastering the techniques that will be presented.

In summary, this primer has two major goals. The first is to assist educational evaluators and administrators to understand the concepts, uses, and applications of cost-effectiveness analysis within a decision-oriented context. The second is to create a basic course of study for those persons who will continue to pursue the subject for more complete mastery. I have attempted to design the primer so that an individual can utilize it as part of an informal course of self-study or in a formal course on the subject. At various stages the learner will be introduced to concepts and their applications, followed by examples. Exercises for each chapter are provided at the end of each chapter to enable the reader to test his or her understanding of the topic that is being covered. Sample answers to these exercises are provided in Appendix A. I have also tried to identify each section and its contents, so the reader can focus on those areas of interest, or return to specific areas that require more concentration.

The central goal of this primer is to introduce the concepts and analyses reflected in earlier works of the author (Levin, 1975, 1981) within an instructional format. Accordingly, a final word on the purpose of the presentation is important. In these days of do-it-yourself instruction, it is appealing to provide a set of mechanical steps that one can simply follow verbatim in order to learn a new skill. Unfortunately, this approach is not appropriate for training in cost analysis and cost-effectiveness analysis. While one can provide a set of principles that can be used for carrying out the analysis, the actual application in any particular setting will require judgments on the part of the administrator or evaluator. Thus, this primer will not be a substitute for a sensitive and judicious effort by the evaluator or administrator in applying his or her craft. Rather, it will provide a new set of concepts and analytic tools that can be incorporated into that activity. While the guidelines for incorporating these new dimensions will be presented and illustrated in this primer, the applications will require careful consideration by the analyst or user.

Importance of Cost-Effectiveness Analysis

The importance of using cost analysis in evaluation can best be seen by considering an example of an evaluation that did not consider costs:

──────────── **Example: Ignoring Costs Can Be Costly** ────────────

In the sixties it was expected that such educational technologies as computer-assisted instruction and educational television would rapidly replace certain instructional functions in the schools. The view was such that functions could be performed "better" or more inexpensively by technologies than by classroom teachers. In 1969 a study was published in one of the most prestigious science journals that found that the use of computer-assisted instruction (CAI) for providing just seven minutes of daily "drill and practice" in arithmetic for disadvantaged youngsters would increase mathematics scores beyond those attainable with standard classroom instruction (Suppes and Morningstar, 1969). Given the difficulty in finding compensatory educational interventions that promised success in improving the learning of the disadvantaged, the finding was impressive. Indeed, the article concluded that computer-assisted instruction had come of age, and it was time for compensatory educational programs to consider the CAI alternative.

The article said nothing, however, about the costs of the CAI or other alternatives for obtaining similar results. An investigation of the costs of CAI at that time found that seven minutes of "drill and practice" per day per pupil would have required an increase in the school budget of at least 25 percent (Levin, 1975, pp. 90-91). In contrast, it was found that teacher-based drill and practice could produce a similar learning effect for an increase of only six percent in the school budget. That is, on a cost-effectiveness basis, the new technology was at least four times as costly per gain as was the more traditional approach. Clearly, a school that used the more traditional approach would have been able to save considerable resources over one that had adopted CAI, resources that could be used for other educational functions or to reduce the tax burden.

The case for using cost-effectiveness analysis is that it integrates the results of activities with their costs in such a way that one can select those activities that provide the best educational results for any given costs or that provide any given level of educational results for the least cost. It is important to emphasize that both the cost and effectiveness aspects are important and must be integrated. Just as evaluators often consider only the effects of a particular alternative or intervention, administrators sometimes consider only the costs. In both cases, the evaluation will be incomplete.

Example: The Cost of School Closings

As enrollments have declined in many school districts, revenues for operating the schools have also been reduced by the states. A large part of the revenues that school districts receive from the state are provided according to a formula that reimburses the school district for each child in average daily attendance (ADA). As ADA diminishes, so do the payments from the state. Thus administrators in school districts must face a situation of cutting expenditures to accommodate a smaller budget — at least when adjusted for inflation.

In all too many cases, the prime strategy for cutting costs has been to close schools and consolidate their enrollments in other schools. On the surface it may appear that this will save costs without any sacrifice of educational quality. However, the cost saving will generally be based upon a mechanical calculation that does not take account of the effects of school closings on educational quality and effectiveness.

Although the cost per student may be lower in larger school units, the educational effectiveness may also decline (Chambers, 1981). Precisely why this is so is unclear. It may be that larger schools are more depersonalized and provide both students and educational professionals with less of a feeling of individual importance and involvement (Barker & Gump, 1964). Whatever the cause, it is possible that larger, consolidated schools that result from school closures may be less cost-effective than leaving smaller ones intact, and there may be superior ways of cutting educational costs than school closures. For example, smaller schools can reduce costs by sharing teachers and administrators and by drawing on such community resources as courses offered by community colleges in the case of secondary schools. They can also lease unused classroom space for such compatible uses as child care, senior citizen centers, and private educational endeavors such as computer schools or tutoring centers. It is conceivable that the cost savings attributed to closing and consolidating schools may be offset by higher transportation costs and poorer educational results associated with sending children from one neighborhood to more crowded facilities elsewhere, while other strategies for reducing costs are left unexplored.

Thus a consideration of only the costs of a decision is also inappropriate and provides incomplete information. In the case set out above, even all of the costs may not have been taken account of. If the additional costs of transportation fall upon parents and students and are not reflected in school budgets, then a major cost element will not even be reflected in the closure decision. The true costs to the community resulting from school closure include even those borne privately by parents and their children in the form of bicycles, automobile expenses, costs of public transportation, bicycle accidents, and student and parental time used for transportation. Even more important is the fact that simply accounting for costs of different decision alternatives — even when all costs are accounted for — does not take account of the effectiveness consequences of the decisions and the relation of costs to such effects.

Both costs and effects must be considered to make good decisions in education and other public endeavors. If evaluators intend the results of their studies to be used for decision making, the information on effects of alternatives is not adequate in itself to make a choice. If educational administrators wish to provide suggestions for cutting expenditures, the cost consequences of the alternatives are not adequate in themselves to make an informed decision. In short, information on both costs and effects of cost-effectiveness is necessary to adequately inform the decision.

Cost-Analysis Approaches in Evaluation and Decision Making

One of the more confusing aspects of incorporating cost analysis into evaluation and decision making is that a number of different, but related, concepts and terms are often used interchangeably in referring to such approaches. Among these are cost-effectiveness, cost-benefit, cost-utility, and cost-feasibility. Although each is related to and can be considered to be a member in good standing of the cost-analysis family, each is characterized by important differences that make it appropriate to specific applications (Levin, 1975). The purpose of this section of the primer is to describe and illustrate these differences.

Cost-Effectiveness Analysis

Cost-effectiveness (CE) analysis refers to the evaluation of alternatives according to both their costs and their effects with regard to producing some outcome or set of outcomes. Typically, educational evaluation and decision making must focus on the choice of an educational intervention or alternative for meeting a particular objective, such as increasing test scores in basic skills or reducing dropouts. In these cases the results of alternative interventions can be assessed according to their effects on improving test scores or on the number of potential school dropouts who stay in school. When costs are combined with measures of effectiveness and all alternatives can be evaluated according to their costs and their contribution to meeting the same effectiveness criterion, we have the ingredients for a CE analysis. For example, alternatives can be evaluated on the basis of their cost for raising student test scores by a given amount or the cost for each potential dropout averted. From a decision-oriented perspective, the most preferable alternatives would be those that show the lowest cost for any given increase in test scores or per averted dropout.

Under cost-effectiveness analysis, both the costs and effects of alternatives are taken into account in evaluating programs with similar goals. It is assumed that (1) only programs with similar or identical goals can be compared and (2) a common measure of effectiveness can be used to assess them. These effectiveness data can be combined with costs in order to provide a cost-effectiveness evaluation that will enable the selection of those approaches which provide the maximum effectiveness per level of cost or which require the least cost per level of effectiveness.

──────── **Example: Remedial Math Programs Compared** ────────

Table 1.1 presents a hypothetical set of cost-effectiveness results for a comparison of remedial mathematics programs. Four alternative methods of improving mathematics performance for low-achieving youngsters are evaluated according to their costs and effects. Although we will assume that students have been randomly assigned to one of the different treatments or to a control group that receives no remedial instruction, it is rarely possible to do this in a school environment. By making this assumption, however, we can focus on the CE results.

At the end of the year the students are tested, and the measure of effectiveness for each of the treatment groups is the difference between their test scores and those of the control group. The four alternative instructional treatments that have been chosen for this hypothetical comparison are the following:

(1) the use of small remedial groups working with a special instructor;

(2) an individually-programmed instructional curriculum (IPI), in which each student works at his or her own pace in a special resource room with individualized curriculum materials and a coordinator;

(3) computer-assisted instruction (CAI), in which students receive a ten-minute session of "drill and practice" of arithmetic concepts, problems and operations;

(4) a cross-age, peer-tutoring approach, in which older students spend 30 minutes a day tutoring the students needing remediation.

The costs of the various instructional treatments are assessed by determining the various ingredients that they use and their values. The small-groups approach shows a hypothetical cost of $300 per student because of its very high personnel-to-student ratios. IPI requires the use of a specially equipped room that stores curriculum materials in sequential files, as well as a coordinator, but a standard contingent of students can be accommodated (for example, 25-30 students) in each setting. The additional costs of providing this approach are assessed hypothetically at $100 per student. The CAI approach requires a special room, a computer and student terminals, a coordinator, and certain other inputs, which cost $150 per year for a daily ten-minute session for one year. Finally, peer tutoring requires some instructional materials and a coordinator, as well as the use of a special room with tutoring carrels. Personnel costs are low because older students are tutoring younger ones, and there is evidence that this activity contributes to the older pupil's proficiencies as well as those of their younger peers (Allen, 1976). Of course, as with the other hypothetical examples, these costs have not been derived from actual data.

The effectiveness of each instructional strategy is determined by the test scores of its students in comparison with those of a control group that has received no remedial mathematics instruction. Again, the results are hypothetical, with the small groups showing an effect of 20 points, the IPI showing 4 points, and CAI and peer tutoring some 15 and 10 points, respectively. When these results are combined with those for costs, we can derive a cost-effectiveness ratio that will show

TABLE 1.1   Hypothetical Cost-Effectiveness Results for Remedial
Mathematics Programs

Method	Cost Per Student	Effectiveness (test score)	C/E
Small Groups	$300	20	$15
IPI	$100	4	$25
CAI	$150	15	$10
Peer Tutoring	$ 50	10	$ 5

the cost per student for a one-point improvement — on the average —
in test scores. While costs vary from $50 to $300, or sixfold, the range
of effectiveness is about five to one, and the range of
cost-effectiveness is the same. That is, while IPI would cost a
hypothetical $25 a point to improve the mathematics performance of
low achievers, peer tutoring would cost only $5 a point in this
hypothetical case. In between are CAI at $10 a point and the
small-groups approach at $15. On this basis, the tutoring approach is
the most cost-effective, followed by CAI.

The most effective approach when costs are ignored (small
groups) is ranked only third when they are taken into account. That is,
for $300 per student, small groups provide an increase in test scores of
20 points. But, at only one-sixth of the cost, peer tutoring can produce
half of that effect. Presumably, a greater use of peer tutoring would
increase test scores at a lower cost per point than reliance on small
groups. Indeed, if additional expenditures on CAI and peer tutoring
were to have the same proportionate levels of effectiveness as the
results in Table 1.1 indicate, then an allocation of $300 to each would
provide a 30-point gain from CAI and a 40-point gain from peer
tutoring. Of course, we would have to assess whether increases in the
intensities of these instructional strategies would have proportionate
effectiveness or would suffer from diminishing returns. A further
possibility would be to combine the present amounts of peer tutoring
with CAI at a combined cost of $200 per child, with the expectation
that the two in combination could outperform the small-groups
strategy at only two-thirds of the cost.

This hypothetical example tends to reflect the situation that
is all too common in actual evaluations, in which the most
"effective" approach is not always the most cost-effective.
Yet, without an analysis of costs, it would be impossible to

know this. Further, the adoption of the most "effective" alternative can actually cost many times as much as the most cost-effective one.

The cost-effectiveness approach has a number of strengths. Most important is that it merely requires combining cost data with the effectiveness data that are ordinarily available from an educational evaluation to create a cost-effectiveness comparison. Further, it lends itself well to an evaluation of alternatives that are being considered for accomplishing a particular educational goal. Its one major disadvantage is that one can compare the CE ratios among alternatives with only one goal. One cannot compare alternatives with different goals (e.g., reading versus mathematics or education versus health), nor can one make a determination of whether a program is worthwhile in the sense that its benefits exceed its costs. That is, even the alternative that is the most preferable according to CE criteria might be a poor investment if one is to ask the question whether the program is worthwhile. For example, it is possible that a program with the lowest cost for saving dropouts is a poor investment in that its costs are still very high per averted dropout, so that society would benefit more if the resources were used in some other way. This can only be ascertained through a cost-benefit analysis.

Cost-Benefit Analysis

Cost-benefit (CB) analysis refers to the evaluation of alternatives according to a comparison of both their costs and benefits when each is measured in monetary terms. A CB study attempts to measure the values of both the costs and benefits of each alternative in terms of its monetary units. Since each alternative is assessed in terms of its monetary costs and the monetary values of its benefits, each alternative can be examined on its own merits to see if it is worthwhile. In order to be considered for selection, any alternative must show benefits in excess of costs. In order to be selected from among alternatives, one would choose that particular one that had the lowest CB ratio or the highest ratio of benefits to costs.

Because CB analysis assesses all alternatives in terms of the monetary values of costs and benefits, one can ascertain (1) if any particular alternative has benefits exceeding its costs; (2) which of a set of educational alternatives with different objectives has the lowest CB ratio (i.e., the lowest ratio of costs to benefits); and (3) which of a set of alternatives among different programs areas (e.g., health, education, transportation, police) show the lowest CB ratios for an overall social analysis of where the public should invest. The difficulties of carrying out cost-benefit analyses are the obvious hurdles to placing pecuniary values on all of the costs and results of particular alternatives.

─────── **Example: Literacy Program Costs Versus Benefits** ───────

Both the strengths and weaknesses of the cost-benefit approach become clearer from the following example. We wish to ascertain the benefits and costs associated with three strategies for improving adult literacy. The first strategy would use a standard classroom approach with some 25 to 30 students per teacher for two-hour classes, three times a week. The second approach would emphasize self-instruction with a number of technological aids, including audio cassettes and programmed textbooks, as well as classes on a once-a-week basis. The third approach would provide three standard classes per week as well as one individualized remedial section with no more than five students.

Let us assume that 4,000 adults with literacy shortcomings are randomly assigned to one of the three strategies or a control group, and at the end of one year a cost-benefit analysis is implemented. Again it is important to remind the reader that although I will constantly refer to an experimental format, there are other methods of determining effectiveness among alternatives (Cook & Campbell, 1979; Cronbach, 1982). While costs will be defined more carefully below, for illustrative purposes it need only be noted that they must include the value of all resources that are utilized to carry out the activity (even if such costs are not found in budgets or are stated inappropriately in the available budget information). Thus, for each group, we evaluate the costs of the resources that were utilized in the program. For example, the standard group instruction program would include the annual value of the space that was utilized, as well as the costs of equipment and materials, teaching and administrative personnel, and any other resources that were required. The cost components of the self-instruction strategy would comprise the

TABLE 1.2   Hypothetical Costs and Benefits of Adult Literacy Projects

Strategy	Costs	Benefits	C/B	Net Benefits
Group instruction	$200,000	$250,000	.80	$50,000
Self-instruction with educational technology	$150,000	$125,000	1.20	–$25,000
Group instruction with individualized session	$350,000	$420,000	.83	$70,000

cassettes, the use of equipment, materials, personnel, and so on. The group instruction with individualized sessions would include both the costs of regular group instruction and the costs of individualized instruction. In addition, we may want to add to the cost of each project the value of the time that the participants devoted to study.

On the basis of the cost estimation, Table 1.2 shows hypothetical costs for 1,000 students for one year of instruction at $200,000 for group instruction, $150,000 for self-instruction with educational technology, and $350,000 for group instruction with individualized weekly sessions. The self-instruction is the least costly because of the lower inputs of instructional personnel, and the group instruction with an individualized weekly session is the most costly because of its higher personnel costs for individualization. If we wish to convert these figures into the average costs per student, we need only divide by 1,000 to obtain the results of $200 per student for the group instruction, $150 for the self-instruction, and $350 for the group instruction with individualization.

How do we assess the benefits of the literacy gains for the three groups? There exist two possibilities. First, it is possible to test the three groups on some set of literacy criteria and to convert the results into pecuniary measures of benefits. For example, given the gains in literacy relative to the control group, one could attempt to ascertain how such improvements in literacy might be converted into improvements in productivity, earnings, and self-provided services. Presumably, persons with higher levels of literacy have access to better jobs and are more productive within their occupations. To the degree that these gains in literacy can be converted into gains in earnings, this benefit might be assessed in pecuniary terms. Moreover, higher levels of literacy mean that individuals can provide for more of their own needs and information. For example, it requires a certain level of literacy to fill out an income tax return or an insurance claim (Weisbrod, 1964). In the absence of the appropriate level of literacy, one must pay for these services, obtain assistance from others, or make potentially costly errors. Avoiding these pitfalls has obvious benefits to the literate person.

A second method of assessing benefits would be to evaluate directly the changes in earnings and occupational attainments as well as self-provided services among the three treatment groups. The problem in doing this is that many of these benefits will not be realized immediately after one year of training, but will only be obtained over a longer period. However, one could obtain data on the earnings of persons similar to the adult literacy students and compare such persons who are literate and those who are not with respect to earnings over a longer period. This is a standard method used by economists for converting educational attainments into monetary benefits (Becker, 1964), and the results could be used to predict the additional lifetime earnings of the present group of adult literacy students resulting from their newfound literacy. The benefits are calculated by taking the number of students in each group who meet the literacy criterion and multiplying times the present value of additional lifetime income associated with literacy for persons from that background.

Table 1.2 shows the hypothetical benefits for each of the experimental groups. The gains in literacy are shown as $250,000 for group instruction, $125,000 for self-instruction, and $420,000 for group instruction supplemented with individualization.

The third column indicates the ratio of costs to benefits for each alternative. In order to consider any particular program, the benefits must be at least equal to the costs. Otherwise, the gains to society from undertaking that alternative would exceed the losses reflected in the resources that are utilized. If the costs exceed the benefits, the activity is not worthwhile and should not be undertaken.

Of the three alternatives, self-instruction with educational technology has a cost-benefit ratio of greater than unity, meaning that costs exceed benefits. Although it has the lowest cost of the three programs, it also has the lowest benefits; in fact, the benefits are less than the costs. This also illustrates why we must be careful not to assume that those programs with the lowest costs are the most cost-effective or have the best ratio of costs to benefits. Both of the other programs show benefits that exceed costs. If we use the cost-benefit ratio as a criterion, group instruction is the preferred approach, followed by group instruction with individualized sessions. In the latter case, the individualized session increases both costs and benefits relative to the regular group instruction. However, the improvement in benefits relative to the additional costs is not quite as favorable as the overall ratio of costs to benefits of group instruction with individualization. Again we see a situation in which the best alternative in terms of benefits is not the best when costs are taken into account.

The final column shows the net benefits per 1,000 students for each alternative. This is derived by subtracting total costs in the first column from total benefits in the second column. Reflecting its high cost-benefit ratio, self-instruction shows net benefits of minus $25,000, because the costs exceed the benefits by that much. While group instruction with an individualized session provides net benefits of $70,000 in contrast to only $50,000 for group instruction, the cost outlay of $350,000 required to generate the $70,000 is considerably larger than that for group instruction. Indeed, if the $350,000 were invested in group instruction alone, we would expect that with a cost-benefit ratio of .80, it would generate $87,000 in benefits.

This hypothetical illustration indicates both the potential value of CB analysis and its potential difficulties. On the advantage side of the ledger, it can provide a necessary condition for selecting an alternative — that benefits must be at least equal to costs. Beyond that, we can assess projects according to how much their benefits exceed costs, either relatively or absolutely. Further, to the degree that other educational endeavors and those in other areas of public expenditure (such as health, transportation, environmental improvement, criminal justice, and income maintenance) are evaluated by the cost-benefit method, it is possible to compare any particular educational alternative with projects in other areas that compete for resources.

The disadvantage of this method is that benefits and costs must be assessed in pecuniary terms. It is not often possible to do this in a systematic and rigorous manner. For example, while the gains in earnings and certain self-provided services attributed to higher levels of literacy might be assessed according to their pecuniary worth, how does one assess benefits such as improvement in self-esteem of the newly literate adults, or their enhanced appreciation of reading materials? This shortcoming suggests that only under certain circumstances would one wish to use cost-benefit analysis. Those situations would obtain when all of the benefits could be readily converted into pecuniary values or when those that cannot be converted tend to be unimportant or can be shown to be similar among the alternatives that are being considered. That is, if the decision alternatives differ only on the basis of those benefit factors that can be converted to pecuniary values, the other aspects can be ignored in the cost-benefit calculations. Or, if those dimensions of benefits that cannot be assessed in pecuniary terms are considered to be trivial, one can limit the CB comparison to the factors that can be evaluated with monetary measures.

However, in those cases in which the major benefits are difficult to assess in pecuniary terms, some other mechanism for assessment must be found. Both cost-effectiveness and cost-utility analyses represent analytical frameworks that do not depend on the ability to represent benefits in pecuniary terms.

Cost-Utility Analysis

Cost-utility (CU) analysis refers to the evaluation of alternatives according to a comparison of their costs and the estimated utility or value of their outcomes. When subjective assessments must be made about the nature and probability of educational outcomes as well as their relative values, cost-utility (CU) analysis may be an appropriate tool. Both cost-benefit and cost-effectiveness approaches require specific types of quantitative data to construct their evaluations. In contrast, cost-utility analysis permits the use of a wide range of types of qualitative and quantitative data to inform the decision. However, the highly subjective nature of the assessments of effectiveness and the values placed upon them by the decision maker prevent the kind of replicability from analysis to analysis that might be obtained with the more stringent cost-benefit and cost-effectiveness approaches. These distinctions become clearer if we provide a hypothetical illustration of cost-utility analysis.

——— **Example: Comparing Programs on Cost-Utility** ———

Table 1.3 provides the results of a cost-utility analysis in which two instructional strategies are being evaluated. Decision makers are

TABLE 1.3   Hypothetical Illustration of Cost-Utility Analysis

| | Instructional Strategy | |
	A	B
Probability of raising math performance by grade-level equivalent	.5	.3
Probability of raising reading performance by grade-level equivalent	.5	.6
Utility of raising math performance by grade-level equivalent	6	6
Utility of raising reading performance by grade-level equivalent	9	9
Expected utility	$[(.5)(6)] + [(.5)(9)] = 7.5$	$[(.3)(6)] + [(.8)(9)] = 9$
Cost	$375	$400
Cost-utility ratio	$ 50	$ 44

particularly concerned with whether or not the two strategies will improve the test scores of students in reading and mathematics by at least one grade-level equivalent in test scores. However, in making an evaluation of the two alternatives, they are faced with two obstacles. First, they do not have the resources to do a formal evaluation of the two strategies. Rather, they must depend upon the information that is available from researchers and practitioners who are acquainted with the approaches for ascertaining how effective they might be. Second, they are concerned with two outcomes — reading and mathematics — rather than a single criterion. Thus, they must find some way to make an overall evaluation that combines both criteria.

Cost-utility analysis enables decision makers to overcome these obstacles by using the available data to make probability statements on achieving particular results, and assessing a diverse set of results according to a common measure of desirability — a utility scale. That is, first, decision makers utilize the information available to them to ascertain the probability of achieving particular educational outcomes with each of the instructional alternatives. In the particular hypothetical situation in Table 1.3, it has been determined that the probability of raising average student mathematics performance by a grade-level equivalent in test scores is about .5, with a similar probability of raising student reading scores by that amount if

Strategy A is selected. In contrast, the assessment of Strategy B is that there is a lower probability (.3) of increasing mathematics scores by a grade-level equivalent, but a much higher probability of raising reading scores by that amount (.8). The decision makers may have come to that conclusion by looking at the nature of the curriculum and teacher strengths, or they may have been heavily influenced by evaluations of the two strategies carried out in other circumstances. The point is that such probability assessments are subjective. While they may draw upon all kinds of information, they are ultimately based upon judgments in the use of that information as well as upon intuition.

The second step is to place relative values on each of the educational outcomes in order to weigh them properly in ascertaining their desirability. The method for doing this is to rate each potential outcome on a scale of utility that reflects the value or desirability of that outcome. For example, decision makers could assess the value of each outcome on a 0-10-point scale with equal intervals, in which 10 represents the highest value. In this particular case, increasing mathematics performance by a grade-level equivalent is given a value of 6, while raising reading performance by that amount is given a value of 9.

It is important that decision makers view these scales as having cardinal rather than merely ordinal properties. Having "cardinal properties" means that equal intervals on the scale are equal in terms of what is being measured so that an additional point of utility at any point on the scale will provide the same additional utility. Moreover, two units of utility represent exactly half of the utility that four units represent. In contrast, ordinal properties of a utility scale are much weaker in that they assure only that higher values reflect higher utility without connoting how much higher actual utility is. Thus decision makers should attempt to rate the two dimensions on the basis of A cardinal interpretation of the utility scale. Presumably, these utilities reflect the priorities for the two outcomes within the educational setting, but we are assured only that they represent those of the decision maker rather than others who might be faced with this choice.

Given the subjective probabilities of the two outcomes for each instructional strategy as well as the utilities or values placed upon those outcomes, it is possible to calculate the expected utility associated with each instructional strategy. In this particular case, that calculation is derived by multiplying the subjective probabilities of each outcome by the utility placed upon the outcome and adding these products across outcomes. This calculation is shown separately in Table 1.3 for each strategy, and the result is an expected utility of 7.5 for instructional Strategy A, and 9 for instructional Strategy B.

Finally, costs are estimated as they were in the CB and CE examples, and these costs are divided by the expected utilities to obtain cost-utility ratios for each alternative. On the basis of this calculation, it appears that there is a cost of $50 per point of utility for Strategy A, and $44 for Strategy B. Clearly, Strategy B has a lower cost-utility ratio, meaning that the cost of a given level of utility or desirability is lower when utilizing instructional Strategy B than when utilizing A. On the basis of these hypothetical results, the decision maker would choose Strategy B.

The advantages of the CU approach are that the data requirements are less stringent, a large number of potential outcomes can be included in the evaluation, and imperfect information and uncertainty can be addressed systematically. The major disadvantage is the fact that the results cannot be reproduced on the basis of a standard methodology among different evaluators, since most of the assessments are highly subjective ones that take place in the head of the person doing the evaluation. Another evaluator with the same information and methodology may derive a drastically different result by using a different set of probabilities and utilities.

Further, although it might be possible to get a more representative panel of clients or experts to set both subjective probabilities of educational outcomes and the values of those outcomes, there are numerous difficulties in taking the utility assessments of individuals and aggregating them to obtain a "social utility" approach (Arrow, 1963). For example, any particular position on a utility scale may mean different things to different persons; that is the problem with interpersonal comparisons of utility. One person may rate an outcome higher or lower than another person might, even though their true preferences for the outcome are identical. Further, there is no perfectly acceptable method of combining individual utility responses into a collective representation, and finally, utility scales are often viewed as having only ordinal rather than cardinal or fixed-interval properties. The latter premise means that a value of 8 on a utility scale does not carry twice the weight of 4. All that one can say is that 8 represents a higher level of utility than 4. Of course, many psychological scales have only ordinal rather than interval properties, so other measures of educational effectiveness may also be subject to this criticism.

Cost-Feasibility Analysis

CB, CE and CU analyses all share a number of properties. They all enable a choice among alternative strategies by obtaining some measure of both costs and results for each potential strategy, so that one can choose the approach that has the lowest cost for any particular result or the best result for any particular cost. However, there is one situation in which estimates of costs alone are important. Cost-feasibility (CF) analysis refers to the method of estimating only the costs of an alternative in order to ascertain whether or not it can be considered. That is, if the cost of any alternative exceeds the budget and other resources that are available, there is no point in doing any further analysis. As a concrete illustration, one might view the situation of compensatory education, in which a specified amount is available for augmenting the education of each disadvantaged child. If this amount is $400 per child, then any alternative that violates this constraint would not be feasible. Cost-feasibility represents a limited form of analysis that can determine only whether or not alternatives are within the boundaries of consideration. It cannot be used to determine which ones should actually be selected.

Summary of Cost-Analysis Approaches

In this section I have defined and illustrated a number of cost-analysis approaches that are used to evaluate educational alternatives. In the remainder of this primer, I will focus primarily on CE and CU analyses because of their rather wide applicability to educational situations. However, the reader should be aware that the bulk of this primer will address the methodology for estimating costs and that this aspect applies equally well to all modes of cost analysis. That is, the differences among the modes are primarily on the effectiveness side of the ratio rather than the cost side.

Outline of Primer

The remainder of the primer will be devoted to a presentation and discussion of the use of cost analyses as well as a description of the principles and techniques for developing such analyses. The next chapter will discuss the decision context, audience, and particular issues that are pertinent to the choice of analysis, its implementation, and presentation. Chapters 3-5 will address the nature of costs, their identification, measurement, and distribution among payers. Chapter 6 will focus on the identification, measurement, and distribution of benefits and effects, and Chapter 7 will discuss the uses and abuses of cost analysis as well as the next steps to take in gaining expertise. Appendix A gives sample answers to the exercises at the end of each chapter. Appendix B has an annotated bibliography of cost-analysis sources.

Exercises

1. Typical educational evaluations look only at the effects of alternative interventions on student outcomes without considering the cost consequences. Under what circumstances would adopting the "most effective" alternative actually increase overall costs to the school district for any specific educational result relative to choosing a "less effective" alternative? Provide a hypothetical illustration.

2. There have been many studies of the relation between enrollment levels in schools and school districts and the cost per student. These studies purport to show how cost varies with school size, and they attempt to determine the enrollment ranges in which costs are lowest. Do these studies meet the criteria for cost-effectiveness analysis? Explain your answer.

3. What are the fundamental differences among cost-effeciveness, cost-benefit, cost-utility, and cost-feasibility analysis? When should each be used?

4. For each of the following situations, determine which type of cost analysis is most appropriate among the following four modes: cost-effectiveness, cost-benefit, cost-utility, cost-feasibility.

(a) A school district wishes to increase the employability of students who terminate their formal education at high school graduation.

Accordingly, it seeks an answer to the question of whether it should expand vocational educational offerings for students who are presently in the general education program.

(b) The school board wishes to accommodate budget cuts by reducing some of the elective course offerings in the high school. A reduction in the budget of $60,000 has been targeted.

(c) A university must decide if it is desirable to establish a new department in computer science.

(d) The state legislature wishes to consider the introduction of computers into every high school in the state. However, it is not clear that the school budget is adequate.

(e) A school district is seeking approaches to improving the writing of its students. Advice is sought from the English department on alternatives. Proposed solutions include (1) smaller class sizes with more stress on writing and more writing assignments; (2) hiring college students with exellent writing skills to assist teachers in grading writing assignments; (3) developing special writing courses for students in addition to their regular English classes.

(f) A community college must reduce its course offerings in the next academic year to accommodate a dismal budgetary situation. The college offers over 1,400 courses in some 38 departments and programs. Enough courses must be cut to achieve savings of $500,000.

(g) Both computer-assisted instruction and smaller class sizes are being discussed as ways to improve the mathematics competencies of youngsters in a particular school district. The administration wishes to ascertain which alternative is preferable.

CHAPTER **2**

Establishing an
Analytic Framework

OBJECTIVES

1. *Identify the evaluation problem.*
2. *Establish the alternatives.*
3. *Determine the audience for the evaluation.*
4. *Select the appropriate type of cost analysis.*
5. *Ascertain the needs for expertise and other resources.*
6. *Decide if a cost analysis is worth doing.*

BEFORE BEGINNING a cost analysis, it is important to establish the analytical framework that will be utilized. This framework consists of identifying the nature of the problem, clarifying the specific alternatives that should be considered in the analysis, establishing the identity of the primary and secondary audiences for the analysis, and selecting the type of cost analysis to use. In this chapter, I will discuss each of these issues.

Identification of the Problem

One of the most neglected areas of evaluation generally is that of proper identification of the problem. By proper identification I mean that the problem should be posed in such a way that the analytic response is an appropriate one. To take an example that was discussed previously, the problem that is often posed by school districts facing financial exigencies from declining enrollments is, "Which school or schools do we close?" The real problem that must be faced, however, is *how to cut the budget in a way that does the least damage to the educational program.* The alternatives to consider include the possibilities of school closure, but they also include the options of reducing personnel, cutting specific offerings, increasing class size, leasing excess space in existing schools, and a variety of other potential routes to cutting the budget or raising school revenues. Narrowing the question to which schools are to be closed is to rule out options that may be more appropriate when cost-effectiveness criteria are used. That is, there can obviously be no cost-effectiveness analysis among alternatives that are not considered.

Identification of the problem must begin with the specific origins of the problem. For example, the origins may be that certain groups of children are not learning to read at an appropriate level. In that case one might wish to ascertain the reasons that they are not learning to read at that level. One possibility is that they need special attention because of learning difficulties.

Another is that they have entered school with reading deficiencies that are not accommodated by the beginning level and pace of instruction. Another is that the curriculum and teaching methods are inappropriate. Each of these causes would require a different response.

Before one begins to address the problem, one must attempt to specify with great clarity and insight the nature of the problem that ought to be addressed. This may begin with a general question of a learning deficiency, budgetary squeeze, high dropout rates among particular groups, school vandalism issues, and so on. Once the general issue is identified, however, it must be pursued in greater detail to ascertain the probable causes of the problem. For example, student misbehavior that is caused by inappropriate rules and selective enforcement represents a different problem than student misbehavior that is a result of racial conflict, a chaotic school program, or serious learning deficiencies within particular populations. It is important to investigate a range of probable causes by discussing what seems to be happening with those persons who have contact with the phenomenon. Only after a careful and sensitive investigation can one identify the problem in such a way that a range of alternative responses can be posited for analysis.

What Are the Alternatives?

The alternatives for addressing particular problems are those potential interventions that might respond to the problem and improve the situation being addressed. It is important to ask whether all of the pertinent alternatives have been placed on the agenda for consideration. Obviously, the classes of alternatives that ought to be considered are those that are most responsive to the problem. Again, this will require a sensitive search for ways of meeting the challenge that has been posed. Although one may wish to draw upon traditional responses as well as those that other entities have used in facing similar problematic situations, one should not be limited to these. In fact, often they may not be the most responsive approaches.

For example, the traditional approach to solving problems of fiscal exigencies has been to pursue directions that would rule out of consideration the cutting of administrative and teaching positions. Instead, the emphasis would be on cuts in nonpersonnel areas such as maintenance and supplies. When reductions in personnel costs have been considered, attempts have been made to restrict them to service workers and paraprofessionals rather than professionals. Consider, however, that 80 percent or more of school district expenditures are vested in the salaries and other benefits provided to personnel. Further, 70 percent or more is generally attributable to the costs of teachers, administrators, and other professional personnel. Accordingly, any substantial cut or restriction of expenditures must inevitably reach these categories. It is just unrealistic to believe that major cuts can be accomplished without affecting personnel.

By ruling out cuts of administrative and professional personnel, the possibilities for budgetary reduction become unduly limited or distorted. For example, a functioning school system needs supplies and maintenance, and a heavy impact on these areas can harm profoundly the educational productivity of a school. It is true that cutting jobs should be avoided when possible because of the human suffering that is created by such dislocations, but such actions can be taken in ways that will minimize harm to the present staff through capitalizing on normal attrition, early retirements, and other voluntary reductions in the work force. When financial straits are extremely dire, reductions in personnel must be considered as an alternative since no major cuts in expenditures can take place without affecting personnel.

A similar concern is raised when one augments the criterion of responsiveness with that of comprehensiveness. That is, not only are the alternatives that will be considered responsive to the problem, but have all of the "responsive" ones been brought into the policy arena? Often both administrators and evaluators will rule out alternatives before analyzing them when such options are politically sensitive. That is, the pragmatic aspects of daily life suggest that one avoid pitched political battles by keeping politically sensitive issues off the agenda if at all possible. While one can appreciate the pressures on both evaluators and administrators in this regard, there are two reasons that all of the relevant alternatives should be analyzed.

First, it is a matter of professional integrity to provide information on all of the pertinent alternatives, while letting the decision-making and political processes eventually choose among them. If those processes are not adequately informed about possible responses, they can never consider the costs and impacts of many of the pertinent alternatives. There is an appropriate place for analysis and one for decision making. If certain alternatives are precluded from consideration by their political sensitivity, then the political and decision processes have taken place before the information and analyses have been derived. Clearly, the two stages are interrelated, but good decision making should be based upon informed choices rather than ones that eliminate potential options before they are ever analyzed and considered.

A second reason for considering even those alternatives that are politically sensitive is that such sensitivity or opposition may be dependent upon circumstances. That is, while some alternatives are indeed "untouchable" in the normal course of events, they may become very vulnerable under more dire circumstances. If a school district is facing serious budgetary problems, it must consider all possibilities that would reduce the budget. If student proficiencies in certain academic areas are woefully inadequate, a wide range of programs for improvement begin to enter the realm of consideration. It is important to consider the strengths and weaknesses or the costs and effects of selecting from all of the pertinent alternatives. It should also be borne in mind that the retention of existing practices is always an alternative.

Indeed, this leads to a final comment on alternatives. Cost analysis is premised on the view that decision makers have choices. The objective is to make the best selection from competing alternatives. Cost-effectiveness analysis and other forms of cost evaluations are done in order to choose among alternatives. If there are no alternatives, there is no point in doing an analysis. That is, no matter how competent the evaluation, it will simply lack usefulness if one cannot do anything with what is learned.

Who Is the Audience?

In addition to identifying the problem and the alternatives that might address the problem, it is important to be clear about the audience or audiences for whom the analysis will be done. In this respect, it is useful to think of a primary audience and a secondary audience. The primary audience is generally the decision maker (and the clientele whom he or she represents) who has requested the analysis. The secondary audience consists of those persons and groups who will also draw upon the analysis.

Since the analysis is being prepared explicitly for the primary audience, it is important that it meets the specifications of that audience. For example, if one is requested to do a cost-feasibility study of using educational television in the school curriculum, it is important to ascertain exactly what is behind the request. Is there a specific technological or curriculum approach that the decision maker has in mind, or is the charge to be concerned with the costs of a wide variety of approaches, from selected courses to full curriculum coverage? These details can be worked out through a dialogue and specification of the issues, and the analysis and report should be written with the needs of the primary audience in mind. They may still result in tension if certain alternatives are placed beyond consideration by the decision maker, even though they may be in the best interests of the constituents represented by that decision maker. Under such conditions an evaluator or administrator will face a dilemma that is not easily reconcilable. This is a subject about which little more will be said, but it is central to the politics of evaluation (Cohen, 1970; Weiss, 1975).

Often, however, cost-effectiveness or even cost-feasibility reports are read by secondary audiences who wish to use the information and study provided in one setting to inform decisions in another setting. If a study will be restricted to its primary audience, one need not be concerned about secondary audiences. However, if a secondary audience is likely to utilize the study, it is important to be clear about what is possibly generalizable to other settings and what is not. An important example is that in reviewing the costs of instructional programs, many cost analyses in one school district do not include the value of resources that are contributed by the state or other levels of government or by volunteers. Quite logically, they include only those resources that are underwritten by local school funds.

For purposes of decision making in the district under scrutiny, the omission of "contributed" resources in calculating costs is understandable. But what if the cost analyses are used by other school districts to choose among potential programs, and decision makers in those districts are unaware of what the real resources are that are required because the report includes only those that were paid for out of local financial sources? Clearly, the analysis may be misleading, since not every other school district in that secondary audience will necessarily have equal access to volunteers and other contributed inputs. Therefore, it is incumbent upon those districts to know the "costs" of all of the resources that are required for any alternative, not just those paid for out of the local district in which the study is done and which represents the primary audience.

The importance of determining which audiences one is addressing and for what purposes is that these data guide the level and nature of the presentation and the types of information and analysis that should be forthcoming. However, given limited resources or conflicts between the needs of different audiences, the top priority should always be given to the requirements of the primary audience. In cases in which the report is not appropriate for other audiences with different needs or in different situations and settings, the authors should be explicit about these limitations, so that the results are not misused.

— Example: Assessing Primary and Secondary Audiences —

The Wilson School District has a large component of Hispanic enrollments. Since many of the students come from homes in which English is not spoken or is not the primary language, it is not surprising that reading scores are low. The state has provided Wilson with special funding for improving the reading proficiencies of Hispanics, but the district must provide an annual report on how it is using the funds and the results of the program. The district wishes to do an evaluation of different approaches to teaching English and reading to students from non-English-speaking backgrounds. Among the alternatives are English as a Second Language (ESL), bilingual instruction, and total immersion in English. The Wilson School District has asked you to do a cost-effectiveness analysis of these programs to make a recommendation on which should be adopted. Before undertaking this task you need to analyze the potential primary and secondary audiences.

The primary audiences are those that must use the results directly for their own decision making. These would include the school board, district administrators, and state education agency, and the pertinent curriculum specialists and teachers. If there is a bilingual advisory council, it would also qualify as a primary audience. An attempt should be made to design the evaluation and report to meet the needs of these audiences. The state will likely set out standards for meeting its needs. For the other audiences it may be useful to interview representatives to ascertain the types of information that they would like to obtain from the evaluation. Since you may have to choose the types of information that will be provided from among numerous requests, you might also attempt to ask each audience to set priorities among its concerns.

The secondary audiences include those that are likely to read the evaluation and that have an interest in its results. These might include the Hispanic population in the school district, educational personnel who are not directly involved in the interventions, employers, residents of the district, and other school districts that may have an interest in the analysis for informing their own decisions. In these cases it is important to provide enough information that the report can serve their needs. Again, it is important to set priorities, since no evaluation endeavor is likely to meet all of the needs of every potential primary and secondary audience.

What Type of Analysis To Use?

Once one has established the problem, the alternatives to be considered in addressing it, and the audiences, it is necessary to select the type of analytic framework that will be used. In the previous chapter I identified four such approaches that use cost analysis:

(1) cost-effectiveness (CE),

(2) cost-benefit (CB),

(3) cost-utility (CU), and

(4) cost-feasibility (CF).

Each has different strengths and weaknesses, as described previously. In this section I wish to provide criteria that are helpful in considering which of these analytic tools will be appropriate. The criteria include the nature of the analytic task, the time available to carry it out, the expertise that is available, other resources, and the costs of the approach in relation to the gains of using it. Each will be discussed in turn.

Nature of the Analytic Task

The nature of the analytic task refers to the characteristics of the problem, the alternatives, and whether the specific type of analysis that is being considered is appropriate. A bit of attention was devoted to this issue in the previous chapter, and greater detail will be provided later in the book. What is important to consider in this context is the fact that some of the modes of cost analysis are inappropriate for particular problems, while others are appropriate but difficult to implement without substantial resources. To take a major example, cost-feasibility analysis would be appropriate only when examining which alternatives might be accomplished within a particular budget or resource constraint. It cannot enable one to choose among alternatives that are within the feasible boundaries according to CF analysis. That is, CF analysis cannot be used to determine the desirability of particular alternatives, only whether they are within feasible resource constraints.

Likewise, cost-benefit analysis requires that both costs and benefits be measured in monetary terms. While the value of additional earnings and employment from an educational investment might be measured in this way, it is not likely that higher test scores or positive feelings toward learning can be meaningfully converted into monetary units. That is, for many potential educational interventions, the use of cost-benefit analysis will be impossible or problematic. Thus, like CF analysis, CB analysis can be used only when the conditions are appropriate, and those conditions tend to be fairly stringent.

In contrast, cost-effectiveness and cost-utility analyses can be applied under a wide variety of situations, and they lend themselves well to providing information that will be useful in decision making. Both permit direct attempts at assessing educational outcomes, either in their own terms (as in CE analysis) or in value terms (as in CU analysis). For this reason, much of the discussion in the next two parts will focus on the CE and CU approaches, while only passing reference will be made to CB. CF analysis requires only an understanding of the measurement of costs.

Time Constraints

In addition to the nature of the analytic task, the time that is available to carry out the analysis is important. Any approach that requires a considerable investment of time to design the study, collect the data, and analyze the data must be contrasted with the time that is available before the information is needed. For example, if one wishes to evaluate the cost effectiveness of different instructional programs for teaching reading to second-graders, it may take a year just to obtain the test score results from the pretest to the posttest. When one adds to that the time required to design the study, analyze the data, and prepare the report, one is probably facing a total time commitment of two years. Clearly, if a decision must be made in six weeks, such an approach is not within the realm of consideration; and, without concrete data on the effects of an intervention, this type of cost-effectiveness study is not possible.

An alternative is to do a cost-utility analysis in which the outcomes will be assessed by a careful evaluation of what is known about each alternative. This information can be used to develop both probabilities of particular outcomes and their values or utilities, which can be combined into a cost-utility study. Such a study may be possible within a relatively short time span, such as six to twelve weeks. Even so, the more time that is made available, the more likely it is that it will be possible to do a full and careful analysis. The main point here is that the time constraint can have a profound impact on what type of analysis is possible.

Available Expertise

The expertise that is available for carrying out a study is another factor that must be considered in selecting a method of analysis and study design. CE analysis can often be done by taking the normal evaluation design and integrating it with a cost component. This means that if competent evaluators are available to contribute to the study, the addition of the cost dimension is all that will be required. Of course, one should bear in mind that the certification of evaluation specialists is problematic, so it should not be assumed that anyone with some training in that area is competent to do the effectiveness side of the analysis. My experience is that a large number of evaluators do not have that expertise, and it is only by scrutinizing previous work of evaluation personnel that one can ascertain their competencies. The training programs and career backgrounds that prepare evaluators are too varied in their content and rigor — regardless of the similarities in titles and courses or descriptions of work experiences — to assure quality control.

Assuming a competent evaluator for the effectiveness portion of the design, the addition of the cost component by someone familiar with that aspect can be done through a team approach. In contrast, CB analysis requires a fairly intricate understanding of the workings of economic markets as well as other mechanisms to provide proper measures of benefits as required by the CB framework. Whether that expertise is available will have a great bearing on the feasibility of using the CB approach, assuming that the evaluation can be cast in the CB framework in the first place. CU analysis also has its own expertise requirements, although these probably are closer to those of CE analysis than CB analysis in their content.

Other resources become pertinent to consideration of which approach to use. If a particular approach requires a large survey of students and schools with a massive statistical analysis, it is important to assure that not only are the time and expertise available, but also the budget and expertise for the survey and computations. In each case, the options for a particular approach and study design must be assessed to compare them with all of the resources required for implementation — time, expertise, and other resource requirements.

Is a Cost Analysis Needed?

Thus far it has been assumed that in most cases a cost analysis should be done; however, this is not necessarily the case. We have already suggested that if there are no alternatives, the entire evaluative situation becomes moot for purposes of decision making. Surely cost analysis does not alter this conclusion. Further, if there is not sufficient time or other resources or if cost-effectiveness types of data will not alter decisions, there is probably not a strong case for doing a cost analysis. However, even when all of the prerequisites for implementing and using a cost-analysis are present, it is important that such an evaluation is worth doing in the first place.

Michael Scriven (1974, pp. 85-93) has developed the notion of cost-free evaluation. In considering the choice of an analytic approach and supportive design for implementation, one must ask what will be gained by finding a better alternative. If the gains will be relatively small, only a small investment in evaluation would be merited. Indeed, if the potential gains of a good decision are minuscule, it is possible that no formal analytic study should be undertaken. That is, intuition and present knowledge should suffice, given that little will be gained from a more formal and extended evaluation. However, when the value of selecting a new alternative can be very great, it may be worth making a large investment in evaluation and analysis. Scriven would say that this situation meets the cost-free evaluation criterion in that the gains from the evaluation will be in excess of the costs of the evaluation. It is cost-free in that more is saved by a good and appropriate evaluation than is expended in resources on that evaluation.

In summary, before selecting a particular analytic technique, it is important to go through a set of procedures that might be summarized by the following checklist:

(1) formal identification of the problem,

(2) consideration and selection of alternatives to be evaluated;

(3) recognition of audiences and their needs;

(4) selection of appropriate mode of analysis;

(5) discussion of feasibility of conducting evaluation;

(6) assessing whether an evaluation is likely to be worthwhile.

Given these decisions, it is possible to proceed to the next stage of the analysis — the design of the study to obtain measures of costs and outcomes.

Exercises

1. How would you seek to identify the problem in the following cases?

   (a) Student test scores at the high school level have been declining for the past five years.

(b) The physics department of a college is having little success in placing its graduates.

(c) A school district faces an anticipated budget deficit for the next year of $200,000.

(d) A university wishes to consider replacing its mainframe computer.

2. Identify a potential problem associated with each of the four situations set out in the previous question. Describe at least two alternatives that might be considered for addressing each problem.

3. Suggest the hypothetical primary and secondary audiences for the evaluations that would follow in each of the four cases.

4. What types of cost analysis (CE, CB, CU, CF) would seem appropriate for each?

5. How would you determine whether a formal cost analysis would be worthwhile?

CHAPTER *3*

The Concept and Measurement of Costs

OBJECTIVES

1. *Describe the concept of costs.*
2. *Show the inadequacy of budgets for cost analysis.*
3. *Present a methodology for measuring costs.*
4. *Identify cost ingredients.*

The Concept of Costs

To most of us, the notion of cost is something that is both as obvious as the price of a good or service and as mysterious as the columns of data on an accounting statement or budget. In this chapter I will introduce a concept of costs that will differ somewhat from both of these, and I will present a straightforward method that can be used by evaluators to estimate costs. Any social intervention or program has both an outcome and a cost. The outcome refers to the result of the intervention. Outcomes of educational interventions include such common indicators as higher student achievement, lower dropouts, improved attitudes, greater employability, and so on. But why are all interventions associated with costs, and what is meant by costs?

Every intervention uses resources that can be utilized for other valued alternatives. For example, a program for raising student achievement will require personnel, facilities, and materials that can be applied to other educational and noneducational endeavors. If these resources are used in one way, they cannot be used in some other way that may also provide useful outcomes. The human time and energy, the buildings, materials, and other resources used in one endeavor have other valuable uses. By devoting them to a particular activity we are sacrificing the gains that could be obtained from using them for some other purpose.

The value of what is given up or sacrificed represents the cost of an alternative. Accordingly, the "cost" of pursuing the intervention is what we must give up by not using these resources in some other way. Technically, then, the cost of a specific intervention will be defined as the value of all of the resources that it utilizes had they been assigned to their most valuable alternative use. In this sense, all costs represent the sacrifice of an opportunity that has been forgone. It is this notion of opportunity cost that lies at the base of cost analysis in evaluation. By using resources in one way, we are giving up the ability to use them in another way, so a cost has been incurred.

Although this may appear to be a peculiar way to view costs, it is probably more familiar to each of us than appears at first glance. It is usually true that when we refer to costs, we refer to the expenditure that we must make to purchase a particular good or service as reflected in the statement, "The cost of the meal was $15.00." In cases in which the only cost is the expenditure of funds that could have been used for other goods and services, the sacrifice or cost can be stated in terms of expenditure. However, in daily usage we also make statements like, "It cost me a full day to prepare for my vacation," or "It cost me two lucrative sales," in the case of a salesperson who missed two sales appointments because he or she was tied up in a traffic jam. In some cases we may even find that the pursuit of an activity "cost us a friendship."

In each of these cases there is a loss that was incurred, which was viewed as the value of other opportunities that were sacrificed. Thus the cost of a particular activity was viewed as its "opportunity cost." Of course, this does not mean that we can always easily place a dollar value on that cost. In the case of losing a day of work, one can probably say that the sacrifice or opportunity cost was equal to what could have been earned. In the case of the missed appointments, one can probably make some estimate of what the sales and commissions would have been had the appointments been kept. However, in the case of the lost friendship, it is clearly much more difficult to make a monetary assessment of costs.

In cost analysis a similar approach is taken, in that we wish to ascertain the cost of an intervention in terms of the value of the resources that were used or lost by applying them in one way rather than in another. To do this we will construct a logical and straightforward approach called the "ingredients" model. Basically, the ingredients model will require that we specify all of the ingredients that are required for any particular intervention. Once these ingredients are specified, a value is placed on each of them. When the values of all the ingredients are added, the total cost of the intervention is established. Subsequent analyses can divide costs according to who pays them and how they are paid as well as other distinctions. In the evaluation setting the cost of each alternative can be determined by applying the ingredients method.

Inadequacy of Budgets
for Cost Analysis

A very common question that often arises is why should we go to all of this trouble to estimate costs? Almost all social programs have budgets, which presumably contain expenditure data that can be used to address the cost issues. Although the existence of budgets is universal, the assumption that they will contain all of the cost information that is needed is usually erroneous. First, budgets often do not include cost information on all of the ingredients that are used in the intervention, since contributed resources such as volunteers, donated equipment and services, and other "unpaid" inputs are not included in budgets. Second, when resources have already been paid for or are included in some other agency's budget, they will not be discernible. For example, a building that is provided to a school district by some other unit of government or one that is fully paid for will not be found in the budget of a school district.

Third, the standard budget practices may distort the true costs of an ingredient. Typical public budgets charge the cost of major rehabilitation only to the year in which the cost was incurred. Thus, when the roof or heating system of a school is replaced, the expenditures are found in the budget for the year in which the repairs were made. Yet, a new roof or heating system may have a 30-year life, so that only about one-thirtieth of it should be charged to the cost of programs in any given year. Budgetary conventions would typically charge the costs of such capital investments to a single budgetary year, overstating the true costs for that year and understating the costs of operating the program for the 29 subsequent years.

Fourth, the costs of any particular intervention are often embedded in a budget that covers a much larger unit of operation. Accordingly, it may be difficult to isolate the unique costs of a new reading program in a school district budget, since the budget is not constructed according to the costs of particular interventions or activities. In fact, most educational budgets are "line-item" classifications of expenditures according to functions and objects. Examples of functions include administration, instruction, and maintenance. Examples of "objects" include teachers, supplies, clericals, and administrators. Not only is it difficult to tie such budget listings to particular activities or interventions, but it is often impossible even to ascertain what the costs are for a given school or broad instructional program such as a language program, since no such breakdowns are usually provided.

Finally, most budgetary documents represent plans for how resources will be allocated rather than a classification of expenditures after they have taken place. This means that, at best, they refer to planned disbursements rather than actual ones. Accordingly, beyond all of their other limitations for cost analysis, budgets may not provide precise figures for actual resource use.

For these reasons, cost analysis cannot place primary reliance on budgetary documents to ascertain the costs of interventions. Of course, these documents may still provide some data that will be of use. However, they cannot serve as a principal source for constructing cost estimates, but only as a supplementary source of information.

The Ingredients Method

The ingredients method represents a straightforward approach to estimating costs. It has been especially designed to assist the evaluator (Levin, 1975). Basically, the idea behind this approach is that every intervention uses ingredients that have a value or cost. If the ingredients can be identified and their costs can be ascertained, we can estimate the total costs of the intervention as well as the cost per unit of effectiveness, benefit, or utility. We can also ascertain how the cost burden is distributed among the sponsoring agency, funding agencies, donors, and clients.

The ingredients method requires that each intervention be described in terms of the resources or ingredients that are required to produce the outcomes that will be observed. Each of these ingredients must be carefully identified for purposes of placing a value or cost on them. The remainder of this chapter will be used to present the methodology for identifying and specifying ingredients. The next chapter will show how to place a value on ingredients to ascertain their costs. Subsequent chapters will consider how to measure the costs of multiyear projects, how to allocate costs to different constituencies, how to use cost information in evaluations, and how to plan the mechanics of a cost analysis.

Identifying Ingredients

The first step in applying the ingredients method is to identify the ingredients that are used. This entails the determination of what ingredients are required to create or replicate the interventions that are being evaluated. Presumably, the evaluation of outcomes among alternative interventions will provide estimates of what those interventions accomplish in terms of particular criteria. Accordingly, the ingredients method starts with a simple question. In order to obtain the effects that will be observed, certain resources are required for each intervention. What are they? Every ingredient that is used to produce the effects that will be captured in the evaluation must be identified and included. Essentially, we are concerned with identifying all of the resources that it takes to produce the effect that will be observed. It is obvious that even contributed or donated resources such as volunteers must be included as ingredients according to such an approach, for such resources will contribute to the outcome of the intervention, even if they are not included in budgetary expenditures.

In order to identify the ingredients that are necessary for cost estimation, it is important to be clear about the scope of the intervention. One type of confusion that sometimes arises is the difficulty of separating the ingredients of a specific intervention from the ingredients required for the more general program that contains the intervention. This might be illustrated by the following situation. Two programs for reducing school dropouts are being considered by a school district. The first program emphasizes the use of providing additional counselors for dropout-prone youngsters. The second program is based upon the provision of tutorial instruction by other students for potential dropouts as well as special enrichment courses to stimulate interest in further education. The question that arises is whether one should include all school resources in the analysis as well as those required for the interventions, or just the ingredients that comprise the interventions.

In this case the ingredients that should be evaluated for purposes of cost analysis should include only those additional ones that are required for the intervention or what I will refer to in Chapter 5 as a marginal cost analysis. That is, both alternatives assume that students will continue receiving the standard schooling services, so these need not enter the analysis. What we are concerned with is what additional or incremental services will be needed in order to provide the alternative dropout-reduction programs. Thus, one should consider only the incremental ingredients that are required for the interventions that are being evaluated.

Familiarity with the Interventions

In order to identify ingredients, it is first necessary to familiarize oneself with the interventions that will be evaluated. The importance of obtaining familiarity with the alternative interventions cannot be understated in cost analysis. In order to know which ingredients are utilized, one must know well the interventions that are under consideration, for it will be necessary to provide considerable detail on the resources that are required. Normally this familiarity can be gained through review of reports, discussions with professionals who are responsible for implementing the alternatives under evaluation, and direct observation of the interventions. Especially important is direct observation whenever possible, for this process will often identify ingredients that would not be obvious from written descriptions alone. The analysis of costs, then, requires an intimate knowledge of the intervention, for it is only in this way that all of the major ingredients can be identified and described in the detail that is necessary for cost analysis.

Specification of Ingredients

The identification and specification of ingredients is often facilitated by dividing ingredients into four or five main categories that have common properties. A typical breakdown would include (1) personnel, (2) facilities, (3) equipment and materials, (4) other program inputs, and (5) client inputs.

Personnel

Personnel ingredients include all of the human resources required for each of the alternatives that will be evaluated. This category includes not only full-time personnel, but part-time employees, consultants, and volunteers. All personnel should be listed according to their roles, qualifications, and time commitments. Roles refer to their responsibilities, such as administration, coordination, teaching, teacher training, curriculum design, secretarial services, and so on. Qualifications refer to the nature of training, experience, and specialized skills required for the positions. Time inputs refer to the amount of time that each person devotes to the intervention in terms of percentage of a full-time position. In the latter case there may be certain employees, consultants, and volunteers who allocate only a portion of a full workweek or workyear to the intervention.

Facilities

Facilities refer to the physical space required for the intervention. This category includes any classroom space, offices, storage areas, play or recreational facilities, and other building requirements, whether paid for by the project or not. Even donated facilities must be specified. All such requirements must be listed according to their dimensions and characteristics, along with other information that is important for identifying their value. For example, facilities that are air conditioned have a different value than those that are not. Any facilities that are jointly used with other programs should be identified according to the portion of use that is allocated to the intervention.

Equipment and Materials

These refer to furnishings, instructional equipment, and materials that are used for the intervention, whether covered by project expenditures or donated by other entities. Specifically, they would include classroom and office furniture as well as such instructional equipment as computers, audiovisual equipment, scientific apparatus, books and other printed materials, office machines, paper, commercial tests, and other supplies. Both the specific equipment and materials solely allocated to the intervention and those that are shared with other activities should be noted.

Other Inputs

This category refers to all other ingredients that do not fit readily into the categories set out above. For example, it might include any extra liability or theft insurance that is required beyond that provided by the sponsoring agency; or it might include the cost of training sessions at a local college or university. Any ingredients that are included in this category should be specified clearly with a statement of their purpose.

Client Inputs

This category of ingredients includes any contributions that are required of the clients or their families. For example, if an educational alternative requires the family to provide transportation, books, uniforms, equipment, food, or other student services, these should be included under this classification. The purpose of including such inputs is that in some cases the success of an intervention will depend crucially on such resources, while others do not. To provide an accurate picture of the resources that are required to replicate any intervention that requires client inputs, it is important to include them in the analysis.

General Considerations in Listing Ingredients

There are three overriding considerations that should be recognized in identifying and specifying ingredients. First, the ingredients should be specified in sufficient detail that their value can be ascertained in the next stage of the analysis. Thus it is important that the qualifications of staff, characteristics of physical facilities, types of equipment, and other inputs be specified with enough precision that it is possible to place reasonably accurate cost values on them.

Second, the categories into which ingredients are placed should be consistent, but there is no single approach to categorization that will be suitable in all cases. The one that was set out above is a general classification scheme that is rather typical. It is possible, however, that there need be no "other inputs" category if all ingredients can be assigned to other classifications. For example, insurance coverage can be included with facilities and equipment to the degree that it is associated with the costs of those categories. Likewise, if parents must provide volunteer time, that ingredient can be placed under client inputs rather than under personnel. The categories are designed to be functionally useful rather than orthodox distinctions that should never be violated.

Finally, the degree of specificity and accuracy in listing ingredients should depend upon their overall contribution to the total cost of the intervention. Personnel inputs represent three-quarters or more of the costs of educational and social service interventions. Accordingly, they should be given the most attention. Facilities and equipment may also be important. However, supplies can often be estimated with much less attention to detail, since they do not weigh heavily in overall costs. The important point is that an eventual error of ten percent in estimating personnel costs will have a relatively large impact on the total cost estimate because of the importance of personnel in the overall picture. However, a 100 percent error in office supplies will create an imperceptible distortion, because office supplies are usually an inconsequential contributor to overall costs. In general, the most effort in identifying and specifying ingredients should be devoted to those ingredients that are likely to dominate the cost picture.

──────────────── **Example: Cost Ingredients for CAI** ────────────────

The principal of a primary school wishes to consider the adoption of (CAI) utilizing computers to provide drill and practice and problem solving in basic skill areas. A consultant is hired who recommends an approach used in a nearby school district. The primary school principal wishes to know what such a system will cost. Using the ingredients method, his staff finds that the following ingredients will be required.

The system consists of 32 terminals connected to a central processing unit with substantial internal memory and disk storage. Each terminal has a video display and keyboard. In addition, the configuration has two dot-matrix printers with graphics capabilities to prepare written summaries of student progress as well as to make graphic presentations for such reports. The central processing unit contains "leased" curricula in three subjects for all of the elementary grades.

Each student session will be ten minutes a day for each subject that is included in the student's schedule. The student will begin the session by "signing in" at the terminal and beginning the lesson that is displayed. Since the curriculum is individually paced, the student will begin where he or she left off previously. A problem will be displayed in such areas as vertical addition, arithmetic problem solving, or word usage, and the student will be expected to write in the answer or to select from among a number of potential answers. If the answer is correct, a notation will appear on the screen and a new problem will be displayed. If the answer is incorrect, the correct answer will appear and a new problem will follow. When a student achieves adequate proficiency for a particular type of problem or exercise — as evidenced by a high proportion of correct answers — the system will provide more difficult problems.

Two types of personnel are required, a coordinator and aides. The coordinator is an experienced teacher who is especially trained for the responsibilities of the overall operation including the scheduling of students; the provision of reports on student progress; consultations with teachers and parents on student progress; security and maintenance of the equipment (such as ensuring that the equipment is working properly and calling maintenance personnel when necessary); and supervision of students in working at the terminals. The coordinator is assisted by aides who monitor the students, answer their questions, and assist them when they are having difficulties.

The implementation of the approach also requires that a classroom be renovated to provide a controlled environment and be secure from theft as well as to provide cabinetry and electrical circuits for the equipment. Such renovation ingredients include the installation of counters, an intrusion alarm, carpentry, painting, electrical work, window grills, and air conditioning. Other ingredients include training programs for coordinators, curriculum rental, maintenance, and such miscellaneous inputs as administrative services and insurance.

The inputs can be summarized according to the following list:

(1) Personnel
   (a) coordinator — experienced teacher with excellent organizational skills (full-time)
   (b) teacher aide — two years of college training and ability to work with students (full-time or could be shared by two half-time persons)

(2) Facilities
   (a) classroom
   (b) renovations

(3) Equipment
   (a) computer — central processing unit
   (b) 2 dot-matrix printers with graphics capability
   (c) 32 terminals with 12-inch video display, full keyboard, and numeric pad
   (d) provisions for maintenance of equipment

(4) Materials and Supplies
   (a) curricula — software for mathematics and reading for grades 1-6
   (b) supplies — paper for records and reports and other supplies

(5) Miscellaneous
   energy (heating, lighting, and power)
   routine maintenance of classroom
   administrative overhead
   theft insurance on equipment
   training of coordinator and aides

Of course, each of these ingredients can be specified in even greater detail according to the precise model and brand of equipment, for example. While space limits the specificity in this example, it is desirable to provide this information in the applied setting. The identification and specification of ingredients must be done for each alternative intervention. Thus, it may be possible to consider a more traditional approach to "drill and practice," namely, teacher-based drill and practice instruction or the use of teacher aides. Given this identification and specification of the necessary ingredients for each intervention, it is possible to place a cost on the ingredients and to calculate the total costs of the intervention. Chapter 4 will describe the methodology for determining these values.

Exercises

1. What is meant by the term "cost" when used in cost analysis?

2. What are the "costs" associated with the following situations?

   (a) It takes a full day at the passport office to renew your passport.

   (b) Your failure to keep records results in an inability to take certain deductions on your income tax.

   (c) The school sponsors an outdoor party for the student body that destroys a major portion of the lawns and shrubbery.

   (d) A rise in school crime and vandalism requires that some teachers be used to patrol the campus rather than teach.

   (e) The birth of a child places heavy demands on your family schedule so that you must defer the completion of courses for an M.A. degree.

3. What characteristics of budgets make them inappropriate sources for estimating costs?

4. What is the ingredients approach to estimating costs?

5. Indicate the types of ingredients that are likely to be required for the following programs. Provide as much detail as you are able.

(a) A peer tutoring program will be established that will utilize sixth-graders to spend two hours a week tutoring third-graders who are not making adequate progress in reading or mathematics. The school will set aside a special room for this purpose and will use parent volunteers to coordinate the tutors and set a tutoring schedule. Tutors will be trained in a ten-hour course that will take place over the first two weeks of school. Training will be done by a teacher with experience in peer tutoring.

(b) A high school is considering the establishment of a fencing team for both males and females that will undertake a full schedule of interscholastic competition.

(c) A school district is considering the establishment of its own program for the education of children with speech and hearing impairments. Previously, such students were sent to classes sponsored by the county.

(d) A principal is dissatisfied with the quality of mathematics instruction in her school. She has discussed the matter with the teachers, and they believe that a combination of a new curriculum and inservice training for teachers will improve matters.

CHAPTER **4**

Placing Values on Ingredients

OBJECTIVES

1. Describe the purpose and principles for determining the values of ingredients.
2. Determine methods for placing values on specific types of ingredients.
3. Derive an estimate of the total annual cost of an alternative.

THE PREVIOUS CHAPTER reviewed the overall notion of costs and the reasons that the types of cost data that are required are not readily available from budget statements. I also introduced the ingredients approach to constructing cost estimates and set out the principles and procedures for identifying and specifying ingredients. In this chapter I wish to place cost values on each of the ingredients in order to obtain an estimate for total costs and for cost components of interventions.

Purpose and Principles of Cost Valuation

Up to this point, we presumably know the resources or ingredients that are required for each intervention. However, the fact that we know which ingredients are required does not enable us to estimate costs. Once again we must turn to the definition of costs as a sacrifice equal to the value of something that is given up by using resources in a particular way. By using the ingredients for specific intervention, we sacrifice their potential use for something else. The cost to us is what we must give up by using the ingredients in this way rather than in their best alternative use. Accordingly, a monetary measure of costs represents the monetary value of all of the ingredients when used in their best alternative use. In essence, it tells us the value of the sacrifice that we must make to use all of the ingredients for this intervention by providing a summary measure in dollars of the value of the ingredients in other uses.

Market Prices

The most common method for placing monetary values on ingredients is that of using their market prices. According to economic theory, when markets for a particular good or service are perfectly competitive, the equilibrium price established by that market will represent the value of that good (Dorfman, 1967). The method of using market prices has two attractive features, availability and simplicity. First, since there are reasonably competitive markets for many of the ingredients (e.g., personnel, facilities, and equipment) used in educational interventions, there will be a set of prices readily available that can be used to determine the costs of those inputs. Second, the derivation of the market price of the ingredient represents a simple method for the practitioner to use in deriving cost data.

Shadow Prices

Unfortunately, competitive markets are not always the only source of ingredients. In some cases there is a market for a particular ingredient, but the market does not meet the criteria for perfect competition. There are relatively few buyers or sellers, or there exist other market imperfections. In these cases the existing market price may be an inaccurate reflection of the cost of obtaining additional units of an ingredient, and adjustments must be made to provide a more appropriate cost measure. For example, assume that a talented program director is presently receiving salary and other benefits valued at $30,000 a year, but there are very few persons who possess such talents. If one wished to ascertain the cost of using such talent to replicate an intervention at many new sites, one would have to take account of the fact that the scarcity of such talent may generate a considerably higher cost for qualified persons as demand for such talent increases.

Alternatively, there may be no obvious market for a particular ingredient. For example, a school district may decide to lend an old facility to a new program. There is no financial transaction, for the building was purchased and paid for a long time ago. Moreover, there is no market that exists for this type of facility. In these cases it is necessary to ascertain what the value of the ingredient would be if there were a market. When attempts are made to ascertain the value of a good that does not have a competitive market price, the estimated value is called a shadow price. Both market and shadow prices will be used to ascertain the values of the ingredients for purposes of cost estimation.

Methods for Valuing Ingredients

When ingredients have market prices, the best measure of cost is that price. The market price is a measure of what must be sacrificed in terms of the value of other commodities to provide the ingredient for the intervention. Market prices exist wherever goods or services can be offered for sale and purchased openly by buyers and sellers. At any particular time, one can purchase those goods and services at that price. Thus, if one can obtain teachers of a given quality at a given price (salary and fringe benefits) in the open market, one can use that price to evaluate the cost of a teacher with those characteristics. The same is true of facilities, equipment, materials, supplies, and other personnel that are purchased in the marketplace. In all of these cases one seeks the market price for obtaining those goods and services.

In those cases in which market prices are inaccurate reflections of the true cost, one must adjust the market price appropriately. In the case mentioned above of the use of scarce talent, an increase in demand will result in a higher price. Accordingly, some effort must be made to ascertain how demand will increase for such ingredients as a result of the intervention as well as the consequences of such a shift in demand on the market price. This is known in economics as "estimating the supply elasticity," but probably most cost analysis in education will not require this adjustment if one is dealing with a single intervention rather than an attempt to replicate it numerous times. In the single intervention case the use of an ingredient will generally not affect the market; however, in the case of numerous duplications of the intervention, demand for the ingredient may increase enough to raise its price.

When market prices are not available, one must use some estimate of what those prices would be, or shadow prices. For example, there may be no specific market for an old school building, but there are various ways that we could ascertain what the market price would be if there were a market. There may be no market for the services of sixth-graders who are asked to tutor first-graders. But, there may be a way of measuring the social sacrifice or cost of using the time of sixth-graders to tutor first-graders by asking what is the value of the sixth-graders' time in other uses, such as learning. For example, what if it were found that sixth-graders who spend their time tutoring learn less than similar sixth-graders who do not tutor? One way of ascertaining the shadow price of their time in tutoring is to estimate what it would cost to maintain their learning achievements at the levels of their nontutoring peers. Each case in which shadow prices must be estimated presents a different challenge that must be analyzed idiosyncratically. Fortunately, the problem is rare enough in educational cost analysis that one will not encounter it very frequently.

Given these overall principles, it is possible to set out methods for ascertaining the value of ingredients for each of the categories stipulated in the previous chapters. Since costs always have a time dimension, one should be specific about the period for which one will evaluate costs. In this chapter I will limit the analysis to an evaluation of annual costs. In a subsequent chapter, however, I will show how to estimate costs when a project must be evaluated on a multiyear basis.

Personnel

Since personnel account for about three-quarters of the total costs of typical educational interventions, it is important to devote considerable effort to obtaining accurate estimates of their costs. The services of most personnel are purchased in the marketplace, so it is data derived from such market transactions that we should consider first. When a personnel position can be filled by attracting persons with the appropriate education, experience, and other characteristics at the prevailing salary and fringe benefits generally paid for such talent in the marketplace, the cost of such a person is considered to be the monetary value of the salary and fringe benefits. This determination presumes that a market exists in that there are many employers seeking such personnel, and there are many people seeking such positions. At any one time these dynamics will result in a prevailing salary and fringe benefits that must be paid to obtain persons for any given position, and that expenditure on salaries and fringe benefits represents their costs. It is important to point out that the price of obtaining personnel in different school districts or teaching situations is also affected by working conditions and other factors (Chambers, 1980). Thus, even though there may exist a general market for particular types of personnel, any specific analysis should take account of observed differences in the employment situation.

The salary and fringe benefits for each person can usually be obtained from normal payroll or expenditure data. It is important to add to each salary all of the fringe benefits, including employer contributions to social security, other pension plans, health and life insurance, and perquisites that benefit the employee, such as the use of a car for private purposes. In many cases fringe benefits packages are expressed as an overall percentage of salaries, since some fixed percentage of salaries is allocated to these benefits. For example, 23 percent of salaries might be allocated to fringe benefits. In such a case one need only obtain salary data and add the fringe benefits based upon the percentage allocation for that purpose.

In situations in which one has data on actual expenditures for particular categories of personnel, personnel costs can be readily ascertained. In other cases, such as new interventions that are being proposed or the use of volunteers, expenditure data that can be used to assess costs are not as obvious. In these cases it is necessary to estimate the market value of the personnel services that are provided. For example, in the case of estimating the costs of a proposed program, one can use data from other interventions or the marketplace to calculate the expected costs for each type of personnel. Likewise, the value of a volunteer can be determined by estimating the market value of the services that the volunteer will provide. Thus, if the volunteer has the qualifications for and will serve as a teacher's aide, one can use the salary and fringe benefits of a teacher's aide to set the value of the volunteer to the program.

In summary, most personnel costs can be obtained by ascertaining the expenditures on salaries and fringe benefits for each of the personnel ingredients. When such data are not available, costs can usually be estimated by considering the market value of the services that will be utilized.

Facilities

In the case of facilities, there are two possibilities. The first is that the intervention will utilize rented or leased space so that its market value is evident from expenditures. In that situation the annual cost is the expenditure on such facilities. When a portion of a leased facility is used for the intervention, the cost value can be determined by ascertaining the portion of the lease cost that should be allocated to the intervention. For example, if 25 percent of a building is being used for the intervention, then about one-quarter of the annual cost of that space should be allocated to the intervention.

In many cases, however, the facilities are not leased but owned by the sponsoring agency. That is, they were purchased or constructed in the past by the school district or university that is sponsoring the intervention. Since there is no financial transaction, how can one determine what the value of the facility is for a given year? The simplest way to estimate that cost is to ask what the cost would be for similar space. That is, although there does not necessarily exist a market for leased school facilities, it is possible to ascertain what space is similar types of buildings might cost to lease.

Usually one will need the assistance of a local real estate agent to make this estimate. In that case one needs to have an overall picture of the amount of space that is being used for the intervention and such features as its age, construction, improvements, and amenities. These can be conveyed to a person who is knowledgeable about the local real estate market to get an estimate of the lease cost for such space.

An alternative way of estimating the value of a facility is to compute its annual cost by taking account of depreciation and the interest on the remaining or undepreciated value. This procedure requires knowledge of three factors: the replacement cost of the facility, the lifespan of the facility, and the rate of interest that is forgone by investing in a building rather than in another investment.

The replacement cost of the building represents the amount that it would take to construct a similar facility. If only a part of the facility is being used for the intervention, one should estimate that portion of the overall facility and its cost which should be allocated to the intervention. Alternatively, one can get estimates of facility costs on the basis of the cost per square foot and multiply this amount by the square footage used for the intervention. Depreciation refers to the amount of the facility that is "consumed" in a year. Essentially, depreciation costs are estimated by determining the life of the facility and dividing the total replacement cost by the number of years of use. For example, if a building has a useful life of 30 years, about one-thirtieth of the facility is "used up" each year. Thus, the depreciation cost would be equal to one-thirtieth of the replacement value of the building.

However, depreciation is not the only cost involved. The undepreciated portion of the facility represents an investment in resources that could have been used in some other way. By using those resources to construct the facility, alternative investment possibilities and their potential income and services have been forgone. These forgone income opportunities can be reflected by asking what rate of return or interest rate could have been earned had the investment been made in the best alternative project. That is, alternative ways of using those resources would have yielded a financial return that is approximated by a rate of interest multiplied times the undepreciated portion of the facility investment.

This is the second component of costs: the forgone income on such an investment that could have been realized if the resources had been used for some other alternative. For example, consider the fact that, had an amount equal to the undepreciated portion of the facility been invested in a bank account and lent out by the bank for some other purpose, a rate of interest would have been paid on this investment. Because of the forgone opportunities represented by the sunken investment in the undepreciated portion of the facility, we calculate the cost to us of that investment of that amount. Accordingly, the second part of the annual cost of a facility is determined by applying a rate of interest to the undepreciated portion of the facility — that is, the value of the facility that remains after taking account of its past depreciation.

In sum, the method of determining the annual value of an "owned" facility is to take the following steps:

(1) Determine the replacement value of the facility.

(2) Determine the life of the facility.

(3) Divide the replacement value by the number of years of life to obtain the cost of depreciation for each year of use.

(4) Multiply the undepreciated portion by an appropriate interest rate to obtain the opportunity cost of having resources invested in the undepreciated portion of the facility.

(5) Add the annual cost of depreciation and the annual interest forgone on the remaining investment to obtain an annual cost.

Although this procedure is a valid one and is used by businesses to estimate the annual cost of facilities and equipment, it suffers from a serious problem with respect to social investments. Clearly, such a cost estimate will depend crucially upon the age of the facilities in that the opportunity costs will be higher, the greater the undepreciated portion. Yet, the value of the services received in any one year may not differ substantially from that of other years, regardless of the age of the building. For this reason, attempts have been made to "annualize" costs by estimating an average of the combination of depreciation and interest on the undepreciated portion over the life of the facility.

Although there is a formula for annualizing the cost of a facility, Table 4.1 provides a much simpler method that can be used by the analyst. Table 4.1 shows annualization factors for facilities with different lifetimes at three different interest rates.

TABLE 4.1   Annualization Factors for Determining Annual Cost of Facilities and Equipment for Different Periods of Depreciation and Interest Rates*

Lifetime of Assets (n)	Interest Rates (r)		
	5%	10%	15%
1			
2	0.5378	0.5762	0.6151
3	0.3672	0.4021	0.4380
4	0.2820	0.3155	0.3503
5	0.2310	0.2638	0.2983
6	0.1970	0.2296	0.2642
7	0.1728	0.2054	0.2403
8	0.1547	0.1874	0.2229
9	0.1407	0.1736	0.2096
10	0.1295	0.1627	0.1993
11	0.1204	0.1540	0.1911
12	0.1128	0.1468	0.1849
13	0.1065	0.1408	0.1791
14	0.1010	0.1357	0.1747
15	0.0963	0.1315	0.1710
16	0.0923	0.1278	0.1679
17	0.0887	0.1247	0.1654
18	0.0855	0.1219	0.1632
19	0.0827	0.1195	0.1613
20	0.0802	0.1175	0.1598
21	0.0780	0.1156	0.1584
22	0.0760	0.1140	0.1573
23	0.0741	0.1126	0.1563
24	0.0725	0.1113	0.1554
25	0.0710	0.1102	0.1547
26	0.0696	0.1092	0.1541
27	0.0683	0.1083	0.1535
28	0.0671	0.1075	0.1531
29	0.0660	0.1067	0.1527
30	0.0651	0.1061	0.1523

*Annualization Formula:

$$a(r,n) = \frac{[r(1 + r)^n]}{[(1 + r)^n - 1]}$$

where r = interest rate and n = lifetime of asset for depreciation.

For example, if a facility has a twenty-year life and the appropriate rate of interest is ten percent, the annualization factor is .1175. One need only multiply this factor by the replacement cost of the facility to obtain an annual cost. In the present case, if the replacement cost of the facility is $100,000, the annual cost would be about $11,750. This table can also be applied to a portion of facilities by determining what proportion of the total facility is used for the intervention. It is that proportion of the replacement cost that would subsequently be used for the calculation.

Assuming that the replacement cost and life of the facility can be estimated, it is only necessary to choose the interest rate. The basic problem in providing advice on the choice of an interest rate is that economists themselves are not in agreement on the subject. In general, the choice of an interest rate should reflect the productivity of the resources used for the facility in their best alternative use (Baumol, 1968; Mishan, 1976, Chaps. 31-34). However, this result may differ among different entities with different investment opportunities. As a rule of thumb, the ten-percent rate seems to be acceptable, since long-term interest rates in bond markets and other investments seem to hover at about that level. However, when alternative investments are especially productive so that higher interest rates prevail, a higher rate might be used, and vice versa. Also, rough interpolations of annualization factors can be estimated from the table for other interest rates. For example, one might estimate the annualization factor for a 12.5-percent rate by taking a value about midway between the factors shown for 10 and 15 percent.

In summary, the annual cost of facilities can be estimated from using their annual leasing cost or rental value or estimating their annual value by considering depreciation and opportunity costs of the undepreciated investment. Table 4.1 can be of great assistance in making the latter calculation.

Equipment

The rules for estimating the costs of equipment are quite similar to those for estimating the costs of facilities. The annual cost of all leased equipment can be easily established. One can also use the rental or lease value to obtain estimates of the cost value of equipment that is donated or borrowed. In the absence of such information, one can use the replacement cost of a piece of equipment to estimate the annual cost by applying the annualization factors in Table 4.1. For example, if a piece of equipment has a replacement cost of $10,000 and a ten-year life, the annualization factor for a ten-percent interest rate is .1627 and the annual cost is about $1627. In general, these principles can be used quite readily to set annual values on equipment.

Supplies

The costs of supplies are often difficult to estimate using the ingredients method, because it is too arduous to set out their composition and price in detail. For example, office supplies may consist of paper, pens, pencils, typewriter ribbons, paper clips, calendars, and so on. It would take enormous resources to list each of these and determine market prices. Also, such supplies typically account for less than 5 percent of the total cost of educational interventions, so that errors in estimating their costs do not create very much distortion in the total cost figure. For example, a 20-percent error in the cost of a category that makes up only 5 percent of the total cost estimate will result in only a 1-percent distortion. But a 20-percent error in the cost of a category that makes up 75 percent of total costs, such as personnel, will create a 15-percent distortion, or a distortion that is 15 times as great.

Accordingly, one might estimate the cost of supplies by simply adding the total expenditures on supplies to the estimated value of those that are contributed. Only in the case in which supplies are a large part of the intervention would one wish to devote greater effort to the details of this category.

Client Inputs

The method for determining the cost of client inputs will depend upon the types of inputs under consideration. Here we are referring only to ingredients that must be provided by clients, such as transportation. We are not referring to fees that are charged to clients, since these represent a payment mechanism that will be addressed in a subsequent chapter. If some educational programs provide their own transportation, it is important to take account of the value of those ingredients, regardless of who is supplying them.

The usual approach to ascertaining the costs of transportation is to include the total expense. For example, if parents must purchase bicycles, protective headgear, and other equipment for their children for getting to school, this can be assessed according to the method for costing-out equipment. The replacement value for the equipment can be converted into an annualized cost through the use of Table 4.1. The portion of use devoted to school transportation can be applied to this annualized value to obtain a cost estimate.

If the parents transport their children to school in a car pool, it is possible to calculate the annual cost based upon estimated mileage and the value of parental time. The major car rental companies make estimates of the cost per mile for operating a car. Since the car is not likely to be purchased solely for this purpose, it is likely to be only the operating cost of the additional mileage (gas, oil, tires, maintenance) rather than a part of the "fixed" cost (depreciation, interest, insurance) that should be considered. At the present time this runs about 15-20 cents per mile, depending upon the size of the car. The value of parental time can be estimated by considering what it would cost to hire someone (such as a school busdriver) to provide this service. That cost in wages and fringe benefits can be applied to the number of hours a year required for parental driving.

If the child takes public transportation, it is the average cost per passenger of the transportation system that can provide the most reasonable cost estimate. Each public transportation system has an estimate of such a cost. Of course, the rider pays only a portion of that cost, and taxpayers pay the remainder. However, it is the overall cost that is required for cost estimation, and the allocation of cost can be made at a subsequent stage.

Summary of Cost Valuation of Ingredients

The valuation of ingredients requires taking each category and using appropriate methods to ascertain their cost values. All ingredients must be evaluated for their costs, even those that are contributed or provided in-kind. There exist particular costing methods for each category in order to obtain an annual cost. Once these costs are determined, they can be added to obtain the total cost of the intervention. This can be divided by the number of students or clients to obtain a per-student cost for the intervention.

─────────── **Example: Estimating Costs of CAI** ───────────

In the previous chapter I presented the case of a principal who wished to consider the adoption of a system of computer-assisted instruction for his school. Accordingly, I described the approach to CAI and identified the ingredients that would be necessary for such a system. The following represent annual cost estimates for each of the ingredients as well as the methods by which they were obtained.

Personnel

The cost of a coordinator was based upon obtaining a teacher with ten years experience and a master's degree who also had administrative skills. This was estimated at $25,000 for the salary plus fringe benefits of 24 percent of salaries ($6,000), for a total of $31,000. The fringe benefits percentage represents the district average for this category of expense. The cost of a teacher's aide on a full-time basis was estimated at about $10,000 a year plus fringe benefits of $2,400, for a total of $12,400.

Coordinator	$ 31,000
Aide	12,400
Total personnel costs	$ 43,400

Facilities

The replacement cost of a classroom is estimated at $60,000. The estimated life of the facility is 25 years. The annualization factor taken from Table 4.1 for a life of 25 years. The annualization factor taken from Table 4.1 for a life of 25 years and an interest rate of 10 percent is .1102. When this factor is multiplied by the replacement cost, the annualized cost of the classroom is estimated as $6,612. The renovations have a life of 10 years and require an investment of about $20,000. The annualization factor for a 10-year life and 10-percent interest rate is .1627, for an annualized value of $3,254.

Classroom	$ 6,612
Renovations	3,254
Total facilities cost	$ 9,866

Equipment

The central processing unit will be leased at an annual rental of $17,250 a year. The dot-matrix printers have a purchase price of about $1,000 each and an expected life of about 5 years. With a 5-year life and a 10-percent interest rate, the annualization factor of .2638 translates into an annualized cost of $528 for two printers. Appropriate computer terminals with a video screen and full keyboard have a purchase price of $1,200 each. With a 6-year life and a 10-percent interest rate, the annualization factor is .2296. Applying this factor to 32 terminals, the annualized cost if $8,732. Maintenance costs for the central processing unit is included in the price, while the maintenance costs for the other equipment is about 20 percent of the annualized cost or $1,852.

Computer — central processing unit	$ 17,250
2 dot-matrix printers	528
32 terminals	8,732
Maintenance of printers and terminals	1,852
Total equipment cost	$ 28,362

Materials and Supplies

The curriculum software can be rented from a software company. The annual rental for three different curricula — mathematics, reading, and language arts — for 6 grades is $204 per terminal or $6,528. The cost of supplies is estimated at about $100 a month or $1,000 for a 10-month school year.

Curriculum rental	$ 6,528
Supplies	1,000
Total supplies	$ 7,528

Miscellaneous

The costs of energy for heat, lighting, and power were calculated by adding the normal requirements for a classroom to those of the equipment. These were estimated to be about $1500 for a school year. Routine maintenance of the classroom was estimated at about $500 per school year, and administrative overhead was estimated at about $1500. The additional cost of theft insurance on the equipment is about $2,000 annually.

The coordinator needs two days of training, and teachers need one-half day of training. Although teachers are not directly involved in the CAI instruction, they need to learn how to integrate that instruction with their own activities. The cost of a trainer for these sessions is about $400. In addition, substitutes must be hired at $70 a day to cover the classes of the teachers who are in the training sessions. Since there are 30 teachers in the school, and each will spend one-half day in training, 15 substitute days are required at $1,050. Thus the total training costs are about $1,450. Training is not required every year, however, since the coordinator and most teachers can be expected to stay at least 5 years beyond the training. Accordingly, we can evaluate training costs as if they were a 5-year investment. At a 10-percent interest rate, the annualization factor in Table 4.2 is .2638, for an annualized cost of $383.

Energy	$ 1,500
Routine Maintenance	500
Administrative Overhead	1,500
Theft Insurance	2,000
Training	383
Total Miscellaneous	$ 5,883

Total Annual Costs

The total annual costs for the intervention can be ascertained by adding the costs of all of the categories.

Personnel	$ 43,400
Facilities	9,866
Equipment	28,362
Materials and Supplies	7,528
Miscellaneous	5,883
Total Costs	$ 95,039

The total costs represent the value of all of the ingredients required for the intervention. That is, this is the cost for replicating the intervention. However, the total cost is not always paid by the sponsor. To the degree that the sponsor can obtain volunteers, contributions, and in-kind services, the cost to the sponsor will be reduced as some of the costs are shifted to others. In the next chapter I will examine the distribution of the cost burden and its implications, as well as the various ways of analyzing costs.

Exercises

1. What are market prices, and when should they be used to determine costs of ingredients? Give an example.

2. What are shadow prices, and when should they be used to estimate the costs of ingredients? Give an example.

3. When a given ingredient is scarce, what is the problem in using its market price to estimate its cost for employing the ingredient in future replications?

4. State briefly how the costs of personnel should be ascertained for both paid personnel and volunteers.

5. How should the costs of facilities be ascertained?

6. Calculate the annualized value of a building that would cost $1,000,000 to replace and has a life of 25 years. Use interest rates of 5, 10, and 15 percent.

7. Make the same calculation for a 20-year life at an interest rate of 7.5 percent.

8. Give two methods for estimating the costs of equipment.

9. Assume that a piece of equipment has a replacement cost of $10,000 and an 8-year life. What is its annualized cost at an interest rate of 15 percent?

CHAPTER **5**

Analyzing Costs

OBJECTIVES

1. Summarize the application of cost methodology with the use of a cost worksheet.
2. Show the distribution of cost burdens among different constituencies or stakeholders.
3. Illustrate how to estimate costs under uncertainty.
4. Address cost estimation for multiyear projects.
5. Present different ways of using costs for decisions.

THE PREVIOUS TWO CHAPTERS explored the definition of costs and the ingredients method for estimating them. We also discussed the identification and specification of ingredients and methods for determining the costs attached to each of them. The purpose of this chapter is to analyze the cost estimates that are derived from this exercise and to place them in a decision-oriented framework.

Using a
Cost Worksheet

Table 5.1 shows a cost worksheet that can be used to set out and analyze costs using the ingredients method. This format enables you to first list ingredients, according to the categories set out in the previous two chapters, as well as their costs. It is based on the procedures that were set out in Chapters 3 and 4. It also adds a new dimension to the analysis by enabling us to ascertain who is paying the costs for each alternative. The importance of this feature will be described below.

Corresponding with the procedures delineated in Chapter 3, column 1 provides for a listing of ingredients. In similar fashion, column 2 permits a listing of the costs of each ingredient as formulated in Chapter 4, and the sum of that column can be thought of as the total cost of the intervention. Thus, the first two columns enable you to list ingredients and estimate their costs.

Total costs are defined as the total value of all of the resources required for any particular intervention. Given our definition of cost, this can be thought of as the value of the sacrifices made by society — the value of what must be given up — to undertake the intervention. Thus, the total cost is the opportunity cost to society of undertaking the intervention rather than using the ingredients for their most productive alternative use.

TABLE 5.1   Worksheet for Estimating Costs

1 Ingredients	2 Total Cost	3 Cost to Sponsor	4 Cost to Other Government Agencies	5 Con- tributed Private Inputs	6 Imposed Student and Family Costs
Personnel					
Facilities					
Materials and Equipment					
Others (specify)					
Value of Client Time and Other Client Inputs					
Total Ingre- dients Cost User Fees Other Cash Subsidies		−( ) −( )	+( )	+( )	+( )
Net Costs					

A school district may need to choose among competing approaches to improving reading scores or upgrading analytical skills or providing students with "computer literacy." The total costs of each of the alternatives for addressing any of these objectives can be estimated by following the procedures reflected in filling out the first two columns of Table 5.1. In many cases, however, not all of the ingredients will be provided by the school district. For example, some alternative may be eligible for support from federal and state agencies. It may be possible to obtain volunteers to staff some interventions, and various costs might be met through contributions of services.

It is important to know not only the total cost of each alternative, but who will pay it among such constituencies as the school district, parents, the state government, federal government, private agencies, and so on. If we assume that the school district will be making the decision, it is likely to consider only its share of the cost burden rather than the overall costs in ranking alternatives. In contrast, the other constituencies that are sharing the costs will be most concerned about the costs to them. Indeed, both costs and effects should be viewed from the perspective of different constituencies or groups that have a stake in the outcome (Byrk, 1983). The ranking of alternatives by each constituency will largely reflect the perceived benefits and costs (broadly speaking) to that constituency rather than the larger societal perspective. For this reason, we must estimate not only the total ingredients cost of an intervention, but also the cost of that intervention for each constituency or "stakeholder."

Before showing how to use the worksheet to distribute costs among those paying for them, it is necessary to emphasize the importance of the total cost estimate. An estimate of total costs provides an overall summary of the cost of an intervention. For this reason it includes a specification and costing of all of the ingredients. When a cost-effectiveness study is disseminated beyond the initial site where it has been used for decisions, it is crucial that all of the ingredients be included. In this way, any decision maker considering the alternative can determine what ingredients are necessary and their costs.

If the study were to be limited to only those costs that were paid for by the initial sponsor, they will give a misleading picture of the true overall costs. Since we can never know in advance which ingredients will be paid for by other constituencies, we should include a complete accounting in the overall statement of costs. For example, some local school districts have no difficulties in finding volunteers, while others have to pay all personnel. In the former district were to leave out of its cost analysis all volunteer staff, it would not be apparent to the second district what the true ingredients requirements and costs will be in a situation in which all personnel must be paid. Accordingly, it should be left to the secondary user of the data to ascertain which ingredients must be paid for and which can be obtained through contributions and volunteers.

Allocating Costs Among Constituencies

The worksheet in Table 5.1 has been designed to accomplish two major tasks. As shown above, it can be used to determine the total ingredients cost for an intervention. In addition, it can be used to show how the costs of each proposed or actual intervention are distributed among different constituencies or stakeholders. The distribution of costs takes two forms: ingredients costs and financial costs. In this section I will review the use of the worksheet to allocate both types of costs to ascertain the net total costs borne by each constituency.

Columns 3 through 6 on the worksheet in Table 5.1 are used to list the costs that will be shared by each of several different constituencies or stakeholders. Column 3 represents the cost to the sponsor. For example, if the sponsor of the prospective intervention were a school district, we would write in the name of the district. Column 4 provides a listing of costs that will be paid by another government agency, and column 5 would include costs paid from private sources such as volunteers, charitable foundations, and private contributions. Additional columns can be provided for subgroups such as different levels of government or different government agencies. Finally, column 6 refers to those costs that must be borne by students and their families. For example, some programs require students and their families to provide books, equipment, and transportation in order to participate.

Distributing Ingredients Costs

The first step in ascertaining the costs that will be paid by each constituency is to determine which ingredients will be provided by each. In this way the cost for each ingredient in column 2 can be entered in the appropriate column 3 through 6 that represents the entity which will provide that ingredient. Of course, more columns can be provided if needed for other constituencies that are pertinent to the analysis. Bear in mind that in distributing the estimated costs among constituencies we are not estimating any additional costs. We are merely allocating the existing costs to the constituencies who will be paying them. This is analogous to first estimating the cost of a piece of property to an investment partnership and then distributing the cost to the different partners. The question of what an intervention costs and who pays for it are analytically separate issues. By accounting for the value of all of the ingredients, column 2 already includes the total costs of the intervention.

As an illustration of this procedure, we can refer to personnel costs. Personnel costs that are paid by the school district would be entered in column 3. Those that would be paid by the state or federal government would be entered in column 4. The cost of volunteers would be entered in column 5, and so on. A similar procedure would be followed for facilities, materials and equipment, and other inputs. A check on the accuracy of these entries can be made by making sure that the sum of the entries for each ingredient in columns 3 through 6 are equal to the cost entry for that ingredient in column 2.

In summary, all of the ingredients can be allocated to the different constituencies providing them. Once these distributions are made, one can calculate the total ingredients cost for each constituency. That is, the value of the ingredients provided by each constituency can be calculated by adding the entries in each of the columns.

Distributing Cash Subsidies

There is one final calculation that we will need to ascertain the net cost for each constituency. In addition to providing ingredients, the various constituencies may provide cash contributions and payments that subsidize the purchase of ingredients provided by other constituencies. For example, students and their families may be charged user fees to participate. In addition, various constituencies may provide cash contributions or subsidies to the sponsoring school district. These transactions serve to create subsidies or cash transfers from some constituencies to the sponsoring school district and require a set of transfer accounts to accommodate them in the cost analysis. Such subsidies will reduce the net costs to the school district and increase the costs to the other constituencies. These transfer accounts are shown below the cost of the ingredients totals under the headings "user fees" and "other cash subsidies."

User fees are any cash charges that must be paid by participants in order to have access to the proposed program. In this case we would add the total amount of user charges to the total amount of ingredients costs at the bottom of column 6 as indicated in Table 5.1. Since these would be transferred to the sponsoring school district, we subtract an identical amount at the bottom of column 3 to reflect a reduction in the net cost that will be borne by the school district. What is important to note is that the total costs represented by their ingredient or resource values have not changed; only the apportionment of those costs among constituencies has changed.

In like manner we take the cash subsidies, grants, and contributions from other government agencies and add those to the total ingredients costs under column 4 and do the same for cash contributions from private sources under column 5 as indicated in Table 5.1. Obviously, since these cash disbursements increase the cost commitments of these constituencies, they will increase the net costs to those groups. Since these are also transferred to the sponsoring school district, they should be deducted from the ingredients cost for the district. That is, they reduce the costs to the school district as reflected in a net total cost for that entity that is lower than the direct ingredients provided by the sponsoring district.

Calculating Net Costs
to Each Constituency

After these cash transfers are noted we can calculate the net cost to the school district and to the other constituencies or stakeholders. These totals are shown at the bottom of Table 5.1 and are literally the "bottom line" in terms of cost burdens for the various constituencies. The net cost for each constituency is the total ingredients cost for that constituency less cash payments received from other constituencies or plus cash payments made to other constituencies. In this way we can derive not only the total ingredients cost of the intervention, which is the overall social cost, but we can divide that into the costs paid by each of several constituencies.

Of course, Table 5.1 is designed to be illustrative. That is, it is possible to do this analysis for any set of constituencies, such as advantaged versus disadvantaged families or different government agencies within a level of government. The most important factor in determining which constituencies to evaluate is to ask which ones have a stake in the decision and will be sharing the costs by providing ingredients or cash subsidies.

In summary, it is important to know not only the total costs of an intervention, but also how those costs are distributed among different constituencies or stakeholders. A worksheet like that in Table 5.1 will enable you to specify ingredients and estimate their costs and the total cost of the intervention. It will also enable you to distribute those costs among the major constituencies so that each of the stakeholders can evaluate its own cost burden for each alternative. Of course, this type of cost analysis should be done for each of the alternatives under consideration. When combined with the effectiveness of each alternative, it can be used to ascertain the relative desirability for each stakeholder of the various proposed interventions.

———— **Example: Determining Who Pays the Costs** ————

The previous two chapters illustrated the specification of ingredients and their costs for a project utilizing computer-assisted instruction. More specifically, Chapter 3 demonstrated how an analysis of the project was used to identify and list ingredients. Chapter 4 showed how the values of these ingredients could be estimated to provide an overall cost for the intervention. The purpose of this example is to use a worksheet like that in Table 5.1 to do a cost analysis of this project that shows the net costs for each constituency.

Table 5.2 provides a worksheet for the project. Under column 1, the specific ingredients that were identified for the project are listed as in Chapter 3. Column 2 shows the costs of each of the ingredients as well as the total cost of all ingredients: $95,039. The remaining columns show the distribution of costs. All of the ingredients required for the project are being provided by the school district, with the exception of one of the classroom aides and the computer. The district is able to get a parent volunteer to be a half-time aide for the project, and a major computer manufacturer is willing to lend the school district the computer that will be used. The result is that the total ingredients cost to the district will be only $71,589, while $23,450 in ingredients will be donated through private contributions of resources.

In addition, the district is able to use a grant of $20,000 from the state to subsidize this project, and it is able to raise $1,000 through a local private foundation that is interested in promoting computerized instruction. The result is that the school district's burden will be reduced by another $21,000 because of the cash subsidies, while the cost to other levels of government and to private constituencies will be raised by a like amount. When these adjustments have been accounted for, we can obtain the net costs.

TABLE 5.2   Worksheet for Estimating Annualized Costs for Computer-Assisted Instruction Project

1 Ingredients	2 Total Cost	3 Cost to Sponsor	4 Cost to Other Government Agencies	5 Con- tributed Private Inputs	6 Imposed Student and Family Costs
Personnel					
Coordinator	$31,000	$31,000			
Aide	12,400	6,200		$ 6,200	
Facilities					
Classroom	6,612	6,612			
Renovations	3,254	3,254			
Materials and Equipment					
Computer	17,250			17,250	
Printer	528	528			
Terminals	8,732	8,732			
Equipment Maintenance	1,852	1,852			
Curriculum	6,528	6,528			
Supplies	1,000	1,000			
Other					
Energy	1,500	1,500			
Routine Maintenance	500	500			
Overhead	1,500	1,500			
Insurance	2,000	2,000			
Training	383	383			
Value of Client Time and Other Client Inputs					
Total Ingredients Cost	$95,039	$71,589		$23,450	
User Fees					
Other Cash Subsidies		−21,000	+20,000	+1,000	
Net Costs	$95,039	$50,589	$20,000	$24,450	

Although the total value of ingredients that will be used remains at $95,039, the school district will underwrite only about half of this amount or $50,589. The state will subsidize $20,000 of the cost, and private sources will subsidize $24,450. In this particular case there are no costs to students and their families.

It is important to note that the net costs and their distribution will be of interest only for the particular application of the project that is being considered here. That is, it is not clear that every school district will be able to obtain volunteers, loans of computers, and state subsidies. For this reason it is important to stress the overall ingredients cost of the project as well as the distribution of net costs for this particular application. "Outsiders" who read the anlaysis should be informed that the net cost to the school district or other constituencies is based upon a distribution of the cost burden as shown in the worksheet. Under no circumstances should the net costs of the school district be reported as the "total" cost figure for the project.

Estimating Costs
Under Uncertainty

At this stage, the overall method for estimating costs and distributing them to different constituencies or stakeholders has been presented. Now it is necessary to discuss certain issues that arise in cost estimation and utilization. The first issue is that of estimating costs under uncertainty. Although we provided a number of techniques for estimating costs, there are two circumstances when special analysis is warranted to account for uncertainty. The first case is that in which there simply is no reliable standard on which to base a cost estimate. The second is one in which there is a range of cost estimates for a particular ingredient.

When No Cost Information
Is Readily Available

In the first case the intervention may require an input for which there is no information on costs. For example, the project may require the preparation of a manual to instruct teachers. What will the manual cost? The best way to address this type of problem is to try to divide the manual itself into subingredients for producing it. In so doing, it will be possible to focus on the process and the ingredients for creating the manual, and the costs of each of these ingredients can be estimated with greater precision than the more abstract task of estimating the overall cost of a manual.

A more difficult example is that of estimating the cost of equipment or procedures that are not readily available at the time that an intervention is being planned. A project that uses future technology will face this type of problem. For example, although the cost of computer hardware may not pose a problem for cost estimation, the school district may need to develop its own instructional software. Such development is not always predictable in terms of the time and other resources that will be required to design it and make it operational. In this case it is best to obtain several independent opinions from experts on the probable costs. Of course, this may lead to the second case, in which there is a variety of different cost estimates.

When There Are Different Cost Estimates

A variety of cost estimates can arise when there is no previous experience on what a particular ingredient may cost. The uncertainty of a new technology is obvious, but the problem can arise even when estimating personnel or facilities costs. For example, a proposal to hire science and mathematics teachers at their market salaries to overcome shortages in the schools would be immediately beset by the challenge of knowing what salary level would be required to attract adequate numbers of such personnel into teaching. A proposal to build a new facility might face uncertainty about some of the structural requirements, a dilemma that can be resolved only after extensive and costly testing of the subsoil. In these cases, it is important to take into consideration a range of cost estimates.

Sensitivity Analysis

The technique for doing this is known as "sensitivity" analysis (Stokey & Zeckhauser, 1978: 233-236). The purpose of sensitivity analysis is to estimate costs under different assumptions to see how the overall cost figures change and if such differences would change the ranking of alternatives. That is, when uncertainty in cost estimation arises, the overall results should be subjected to an analysis that ascertains how sensitive the conclusions are to the assumptions. There are at least two systematic ways of doing this.

The simplest method is to take each ingredient characterized by uncertainty in cost and determine what types of assumptions would affect costs. Then use the different assumptions to ascertain the range of costs that are possible. Based upon this set of costs, select a high value, a low value, and a medium value. The high value would be the value under the most costly assumptions, while the low value would be that under the least costly assumptions. The medium value can be thought of as the most probable result, which can be the midpoint between the two extremes or some middle estimate that is based upon the most probable assumption.

This procedure should be repeated for each of the ingredients whose costs are uncertain. When the costs are totaled and distributed to the constituencies there will be a high estimate, low estimate, and a most probable estimate for total costs and net costs to each stakeholder. This should be done for each alternative under consideration. Finally, the sensitivity analysis is carried out by using the different cost estimates for each alternative in comparing their estimated cost-effectiveness. The main concern is to see if the ranking of alternatives changes when cost assumptions change. For example, it may be that a ranking of projects according to their cost-effectiveness is invariant with regard to different cost assumptions. In this case the sensitivity analysis will suggest that the results are highly robust with respect to different assumptions in estimating costs. If, however, the ranking of projects changes with different assumptions, it will be necessary to decide among alternatives by deciding which assumptions seem most reasonable.

In any case, it is important to inform decision makers about whether the results are robust or not under different assumptions about costs. It is also important to note that the problem of uncertainty does not always raise itself in a serious way. For many interventions, it is possible to get a reasonably accurate picture of costs without worrying about a sensitivity analysis. Thus the analyst should do a sensitivity analysis only when it is clearly warranted.

Multiyear Projects

I have stressed that any cost analysis must always be referenced to a time period. That is, we are concerned with what the costs (and benefits, effects, or utility) of an intervention are for a particular period of time. Since educational programs are typically planned on an annual basis, a period of a year has been used as a basis for estimating costs. Indeed, I have emphasized the procedure of annualizing the cost of facilities and equipment in Chapter 4. The cost analysis approach that was developed will make it possible to compare costs among alternatives on an annual basis. There are two situations, however, in which one may wish to depart from the single-year comparison. The first is when one wishes to know the costs of a project in a subsequent year as a result of inflation. The second is when one wishes to determine the "entire" cost of an intervention over its projected life. A related issue is how one analyzes the distribution of costs in multiyear projects.

Adjusting Costs
for Inflation

For each year of a multiyear project, it is possible to undertake an ingredients analysis and to estimate the costs of each ingredient. However, this analysis will not take account of the fact that costs may be higher in future years because of inflation. If one wishes to know the cost of the intervention for the following year, it is important to make some adjustment for changes in cost levels. The simplest way of doing this is to assume that the increase in costs, on the average, will reflect the general rate of increase in prices. For example, if consumer prices are expected to rise about five percent a year, each subsequent year should reflect a rate of price increase that is calculated at five percent over the previous year. Information on the anticipated rate of inflation can generally be derived from state and federal government agencies such as the U.S. Departments of Labor and Commerce. Many of the major banks also make such forecasts.

A more complex way of adjusting costs for inflation is to provide different rates of cost change for different ingredients on the basis of trends. For example, although personnel and facilities costs may rise over time, they often rise at different rates. Information on what has happened in the last five years in a local situation is informative. For example, data on changes in personnel salaries and fringe benefits are available from local educational agencies, and information on facilities costs can be obtained from local real estate representatives. In some cases, equipment costs may be declining, such as those of microcomputers. However, the purchase of equipment or its long-term lease will tend to "lock in" a particular cost, which precludes taking advantage of future cost reductions.

Although estimating the costs for future years on an ingredient-by-ingredient basis is both more sophisticated and more complex, it is usually not necessary. The reason is that an overall estimate of cost increase such as that reflected in the wholesale price index (WPI) or consumer price index (CPI) is probably sufficient for approximating what will happen to costs. Further, it should be borne in mind that inflation will affect all of the competing alternatives. Accordingly, all will be subject to the same trend in cost increases over time, so that inflation is not likely to change the ranking of alternatives in the eventual CE, CB, or CU analysis. Indeed, only in the case in which there are massive differences in composition among the types of ingredients will the more complex approach provide overall rates of cost increases that differ among projects. The main advantage of adjusting cost estimates for subsequent years by potential cost increases is that a more accurate picture of future resources requirements can be used for cost feasibility and planning.

Overall Costs of Multiyear Projects

The focus on the annual cost of an intervention is consistent with the operation of schools. That is, a change in an educational program is usually one that will continue for the foreseeable future if it is judged to be meritorious. Accordingly, a cost analysis that provides comparisons among alternatives on an annual basis is highly appropriate. There may be circumstances, however, in which the appropriate comparison should focus on a multiyear comparison of costs.

─────── **Example: Costing a Computerized Curriculum** ───────

A school district is faced with two alternative approaches to implementing a computerized curriculum. Both alternatives would entail phasing in computerized courses over all of the grade levels, beginning with grades 11 and 12 and proceeding to the previous grades over a six-year period. Thus the second year would add grades 9 and 10, the third year would add 7 and 8, and so on.

The first alternative would entail the purchase of additional microcomputers for each of the five years to accommodate the expansion of the curriculum. Each microcomputer would be connected through a network to a large central storage device that would hold the curricula for two grade levels. However, the actual operations for each student would be located in his or her microcomputer, and each year the school district would purchase enough new microcomputers to accommodate the additional grades that would be included.

The second alternative would entail the use of a large central processing unit with substantial memory for storing curricula and programs. The central processing unit would be purchased in the first year. Student access to the central computer would be achieved through the use of computer terminals that lack the capabilities of the microcomputers, since all of the memory and operational capacity would be in the central processing unit. Although the central processing unit would be costly, each computer terminal would cost only about 25 percent as much as a microcomputer. Each year the school district would purchase or lease enough new terminals to accommodate additional students.

It is assumed that the two systems will have the same operational capacity for delivering instruction, so that the effectiveness should not differ. That is, each student will have the same amount of access to the same curriculum with the same computer capabilities for taking instruction. The basic differences between the two alternatives are reflected in possible differences in costs. The microcomputer approach does not require the large initial investment in a central processing unit, but the costs for each microcomputer will be considerably greater than the costs of computer terminals that can be used with the central processing unit.

The comparison is further complicated by the fact that a comparison of costs in any one year will be unrepresentative of the total cost over the twelve-year period for which the project is planned. The first alternative would require phasing in the costs rather evenly over a six-year period, while the second would require the purchase of an expensive central processing unit and installation in the first year, with only smaller increments in costs over subsequent years for acquiring the relatively inexpensive terminals.

How should we do the cost analysis? The natural inclination might be to add up the costs of each alternative for the six years of the developmental period to see which is greater. This solution has two deficiencies. First, the project is likely to last considerably more than six years, since that is only the development period. We are also concerned with expected differences in costs when the project is fully developed. Accordingly, we would probably want to examine the costs over the expected life of the project, which we will assume is twelve years in this example. A second problem is that the cost to the school district will depend not only on what the alternative costs are in a given year, but on when the costs are incurred.

The underlying issues can be seen more clearly if we take a simple example of three expenditure patterns over a five-year period. As shown in Table 5.3, where these patterns are illustrated, in all three cases the total expenditure is $1000. However, in the case of A the entire amount is spent in the first year, while in the case of B the amount is composed of equal annual payments of $200. In the case of C the entire amount is spent in

TABLE 5.3   Three Alternative Expenditure Patterns

Year	Individual A	Individual B	Individual C
1	$1000	200	—
2	—	200	—
3	—	200	—
4	—	200	—
5	—	200	$1000
Total	$1000	$1000	$1000
Present Value (r = .10)	$1000	$834	$683

$$PV = \sum_{t=1}^{5} \frac{C}{(1+r)^{t-1}}$$

the last year. From the perspective of the sacrifice principle of costs, individual B has incurred a lower cost than individual A, because he has the use of some of his money for almost all of the five-year period. Individual C has the lowest cost of all, since her expenditure pattern permits her to use the entire amount in the first four years, sacrificing it only in the final year of the period. In contrast, individual A must give up all of his $1000 in the first year. The result is that individual A must sacrifice more value in alternative opportunities than does individual B or C, even though the total outlay of each over a five-year period is $1000.

This can be seen more clearly if we look at year 2. Individual A has relinquished $1000 and must sacrifice $1000 in alternatives. However, individual B has relinquished only $200 and can use the other $800. For example, if individual B were to put the $800 into a one-year treasury note at an interest rate of ten percent, he would realize an additional $80 in income for that year. Clearly, the expenditure pattern represented for individual B would leave him better off than individual A. In the case of C, she could earn the ten percent for each of the first four years and receive $100 of additional income each year.

Thus, even though each person is making an outlay of $1000 over the five-year period, the value of the outlay is most costly to A and least costly to C.

The principle embedded in this example also holds when we ascertain the costs of multiyear projects for social entities. In general, the more that we are able to defer costs until the latter part of the investment period, the lower the sacrifice, or "real" costs, to the entity. The method for doing this is to compare alternative investment patterns by calculating their present values in a way that reduces the impact of future expenditures relative to current ones. This procedure takes account of the fact that deferring costs enables one to have access to resources for a longer period. Thus the present value tends to neutralize differences in the time pattern of allocations when adding up the cost outlays for a multiyear project.

The calculation of present value uses an interest rate to discount future costs relative to current ones. Although the formulation of the procedure differs slightly from the one used here, Mishan (1976, Chap. 27) provides an excellent brief discussion of the present value calculation. (This method is also used to compare benefits patterns over time, where some investments provide benefits immediately and others defer them until farther into the future.) The formula for estimating the present value of a future cost outlay is

$$PV = C/(1 + r)^{t-1}$$

In this formulation PV stands for present value; C denotes the cost, r denotes the discount rate, which is a rate of interest used to reduce the present value of a deferred cost; and t is the year in which the cost outlay will be made, where t is equal to 1 for this year, 2 for next year, 3 for the following year, and so on. To show how to use the formula, we can take as an example the outlay of $1000 in year 5, as reflected in the expenditure pattern of individual C in Table 5.3 and use a discount rate of ten percent, which was the rate of interest that was suggested in Chapter 4:

$$PV = \$1000/(1 + .10)^4 = \$1000/(1.10)^4 = \$1000/1.464 = \$683$$

On the basis of this calculation it appears that the present value of a $1000 disbursement made five years hence at a discount rate of ten percent is about $683. If a lower discount rate were used, such as five percent, the present value would be $823, reflecting the lower opportunity cost attached to using the resources at an earlier time. A discussion of the criteria for choosing a discount rate can be found in Mishan (1976, Chaps. 30-34). More generally, the present value of any time pattern of expenditure can be found by using the expression:

$$PV = \sum_{t=1}^{n} C/(1 + r)^{t-1}$$

where

$$(t = 1,2,...,n)$$

When this expression is applied to the five-year expenditure patterns of individuals A, B, and C with a ten-percent discount rate, one finds that the present value of the cost for A is $1000, for B it is $834, and for C it is $683. That is, C has the lowest sacrifice in costs, even though she too spends $1000 over the five-year period.

We can apply the present value procedure to the choice of computer equipment set out above by determining the costs incurred for each of the twelve years of the anticipted project, *without annualizing the costs*. We would then calculate the present value of the twelve-year stream of cost for each alternative. The one with the lowest present value would be the least costly.

Cost Distribution on Multiyear Projects

A final concern about multiyear projects is that the cost distribution might change over time. That is, in the early years the sponsor might receive grants from foundations or government in order to provide an incentive for a new approach. At some future time, however, this assistance might be withdrawn as the contributing agency turns its attentions in other directions. For this reason it is important to review carefully the allocation of ingredients and cash subsidies provided by other constituencies to the sponsoring one to see if they hold for the period of analysis. If it is likely that some of them may be reduced or increased in subsequent years, these changes should be taken into account in considering the costs to each stakeholder or constituency and in using that information to assess priorities among competing alternatives.

Costs and Decisions

A final set of issues relating to the use of costs in decisions is how to integrate cost analysis and cost-effectiveness analysis with the decision framework. As demonstrated above, it is possible to determine overall social costs of an intervention as well as the costs to the sponsor and to other constituencies. In general, the type of decision that will be made as well as who will make it will determine which cost figure will be pertinent. For example, if we do a national study to ascertain the most efficient way to raise computer literacy, we may wish to rely on the total ingredients costs of the alternatives as well as their effectiveness. The reason that we would choose the total ingredients costs is that from a national perspective we are usually concerned with the most efficient deployment of national resources, rather than the cost to particular constituencies. Of course, even at the national level we might have some concern about how the burden would be shared between the federal government and the states or between the public and private sectors.

As pointed out above, however, each constituency or stakeholder will typically be concerned with the costs to its members (and the benefits or results for its members) rather than the overall ingredients costs. Thus a local school district, a state, or a parent group would normally wish to assess the costs of and benefits or effectiveness of each alternative for its constituents. Indeed, each constituency may rank the same alternatives differently if the distribution of costs and effects differs among them. Thus a major dimension of cost analysis from the decision perspective is to consider who is making the decision or on whose behalf the decision is being made.

A second set of issues revolves around the nature of the decision. Let us take three types of decision questions:

1. In reviewing a number of alternatives, are all of them within the realm of cost-feasibility?

2. Are there "add-on" or incremental programs that ought to be considered to improve an educational outcome?

3. Which program has the best average outcome per student relative to the per-student cost?

The first question refers to the area of cost-feasibility and the issue of whether the decision maker has adequate resources to consider the alternative. In this case the potential educational outcomes are not taken into consideration. The only issue is whether the alternative is feasible from the cost perspective. The answer to that question is determined by comparing the total cost requirements and those for each constituency with the resource constraints of each for every alternative. Alternatives that require greater cost outlays than those that are available, in total or for the various constituencies, are probably not feasible. Thus, cost feasibility analysis simply determines which alternatives are within the boundaries of further consideration.

The second question arises when the decision maker wants to know if an ongoing program should be expanded or if some type of special program should be added to existing offerings. In this case we are not concerned with developing and analyzing the costs of the existing program. We are interested only in doing a cost-effectiveness analysis of the additional increment or add-on. This is known as marginal cost analysis, since the cost-effectiveness analysis will only be done on the additional resources required or the marginal ingredients. This type of situation arises when a school is interested in considering ways of improving a learning outcome such as reading. One alternative might be to reduce class size, while a second might be to hire additional remedial specialists. A third alternative could be the use of computers or audiovisual aids. We are concerned then with comparing the costs of each of these add-on programs and the effects that they will have on raising reading scores. The analysis is limited to the additional costs and the additional results that are associated with each intervention rather than the overall costs of reading instruction in the school and the overall reading scores. Therefore our analysis is called a marginal cost (and effectiveness) analysis, since we are concerned only with evaluations of the potential additional costs and effects of the alternatives.

The most typical question raised is reflected in the third question. Which alternative has the best educational result per student relative to its cost per student? The actual comparison of alternatives with respect to their desirability is determined by dividing the cost by the number of students who will be served (per-student cost) and obtaining a measure of effectiveness on a per-student basis (e.g., average rise in test scores). We can view this as an analysis of average cost effectiveness of each alternative, since the data are averaged on a per-student basis.

Thus we may conclude in a particular situation, as reflected in Table 1.1, that peer tutoring is a better alternative than other instructional interventions, because it has the lowest cost per point of test score gain. This type of comparison is quite prevalent and is usually satisfactory, with one major qualification. Average cost-effectiveness results are often sensitive to the scale of the application, such that the most cost-effective alternative for a small-scale implementation is not the most cost-effective one for a large-scale implementation.

The problem of scale arises because some interventions have a large component of "fixed costs," while others do not. Fixed costs refer to these ingredients that are relatively invariant, regardless of the number of students who are using them. Often interventions with high fixed costs require a large investment even when the number of students served is very modest. For example, many technology-based interventions have large components of fixed costs. The installation of closed-circuit television in a school will require a large investment whether the technology is used widely for instruction or whether it is used only in a limited way. This means that when that fixed cost is apportioned over relatively few students and courses, its per-student cost will be very high. When apportioned over large numbers of students, however, the per-student cost may be very low (Jamison, Klees, & Wells, 1978).

In contrast, other interventions may have low components of fixed costs and be characterized by high components of variable costs. Variable costs refer to the costs of those ingredients that must be increased as enrollments increase. That is, they vary with enrollments. Teacher-based alternatives tend to have a large component of variable costs and low fixed costs. At low enrollment levels few teachers are needed, while at higher enrollment levels more teachers are needed. In contrast, the cost requirements for a closed-circuit television system for a school will be relatively invariant with respect to enrollments, because of the high component of fixed costs.

For this reason a comparison of cost-effectiveness of alternatives on a per-student basis must take account of the scale of the application. Interventions with a high component of fixed costs tend to be very costly on a per-student basis for programs with low enrollments relative to those with low components of fixed costs and high components of variable costs. At very high levels of enrollments, however, the fixed costs are divided over more students and often become considerably less costly than programs characterized by large variable costs. As more students are enrolled, costs do not increase commensurately, since the same fixed investment can be used for more and more students.

The result is that cost-effectiveness findings for one level of enrollments may not be the same for higher or lower levels of enrollments. This means that a sensitivity analysis should be done over the range of enrollments that might be considered for the alternatives, and results of other studies that are being reviewed should be scrutinized for the enrollment levels on which they are based.

Summary

This chapter has addressed the analysis of cost information by showing how such data can be developed through the use of a worksheet and how the cost burdens can be analyzed among different constituencies or stakeholders. In addition, a technique for addressing cost estimation under uncertainty was presented, namely, sensitivity analysis. Finally, the chapter discussed the use of different cost measures for different types of decisions. The next section of the primer will address the measurement and integration of benefits, effects, and utility with the cost analysis.

Exercises

1. Your school district is considering a dropout prevention program for high school youth. Two alternative programs have been suggested. Program A would expand the counseling program of the school to provide additional services to potential dropouts. On the basis of the characteristics of past dropouts, a profile of potential dropouts would be developed. These potential dropouts would be placed in counseling and guidance groups. Program B would place potential dropout students in part-time jobs. An employment registry would be established in the school, and employers in the community would be asked to provide part-time jobs. Using worksheets like those in Table 5.1, develop a list of hypothetical ingredients for each alternative. How would you estimate the costs of each ingredient? That is, what procedures would you use? Provide some hypothetical costs that might be derived from these procedures.

2. For Program A you are able to obtain a subsidy from the federal government of $10,000 under a program for disadvantaged children. For program B you are able to obtain volunteers to run the employment registry and to solicit jobs in the community. In addition, you are able to get a private foundation to contribute $5000 for program B. Show how you would use these data to distribute the cost burden among the various constituencies.

3. Assume that you do a cost-effectiveness analysis of different alternatives, in which you use the total ingredients cost (on a per-student basis) as well as a student-based outcome as a measure of effectiveness. Based upon this analysis you are able to rank the alternatives according to their cost-effectiveness. Under what circumstances might a decision maker rationally choose an alternative different from the one that you have ranked as being the most cost-effective?

4. For what types of ingredients might costs be most uncertain? Can you give some specific illustrations? How would you do a sensitivity analysis for these ingredients, and how would you incorporate it into the overall comparison of alternatives?

5. In order to predict annual costs for an intervention for each of the next several years, what modifications would you make to the cost values that are estimated for this year?

6. It is possible to compare the costs of alternatives by estimating their overall costs over a multiyear period rather than following the more conventional approach of estimating their annual costs. Why is it not acceptable to simply obtain the sum of the annual costs to derive the multiyear costs?

7. What is the conceptual basis for using a present-value calculation to compare costs of multiyear alternative projects?

8. Assume that you are asked to review the costs of a seven-year project. After doing a careful identification and specification of ingredients and their costs, you obtain the following costs:

Year 1	$ 11,000
Year 2	13,000
Year 3	18,500
Year 4	10,800
Year 5	27,000
Year 6	23,000
Year 7	21,000

Use the expression in this chapter to derive the present value of this stream of costs for both a five-percent and a ten-percent discount rate. Compare the present values obtained by these calculations with a simple summation of the costs for the seven years. Why do they differ?

9. How would you use the cost information generated in Table 5.1 to determine if a set of alternatives is feasible from a cost perspective?

10. Under what circumstances should your cost analysis and effectiveness analysis be based on marginal costs and effects? Provide an example.

11. Assume that you derive cost-effectiveness results for a group of alternative interventions for a single school. The school district wants to know if the same cost-effectiveness findings are applicable for the entire school district. Discuss the issues involved in answering this question from the perspective of the cost analysis.

CHAPTER 6

Benefits, Effects, and Utility

OBJECTIVES

1. Address the formulation of benefits and their measurement.
2. Address the formulation of effectiveness and its measurement.
3. Present cost-utility concepts and their measurement.
4. Discuss the treatment of multiple outcomes.
5. Provide an understanding of the possibilities for distributing benefits and effects.

COST ANALYSIS in evaluation must always consider both the results and costs of interventions. By comparing both costs and results among alternatives, one can choose the alternative that provides the best results for any given cost outlay or that minimizes the cost for any given result. In previous chapters the assessment of costs and their measurement were presented. In this chapter the assessment of results is addressed in the form of benefits, effects, and utility.

In a certain sense this will appear to be a case of déjà vu for evaluators, for the heart of the evaluation exercise is often precisely that of ascertaining the effects of interventions on particular criteria. For example, evaluators often face situations in which they are asked to ascertain the impact of alternative curricula on reading scores or the effects of a teacher retraining program on teacher performance. In this respect, the evaluation of outcomes is a familiar endeavor, and it is hardly the purpose of this manual to review basic evaluation approaches. But there are certain aspects of assessment of results that are either unique to cost-analysis approaches or that become more prominent when such approaches are used. This chapter reviews these issues.

The first chapter reviewed four different approaches to assessing the results of alternatives: benefits, effectiveness, utility, and feasibility. In the second chapter I suggested criteria to consider in using them. In this chapter I wish to scrutinize benefits, effectiveness, and utility meaures more closely to understand how they might be used and implemented.

Benefits and
Their Measurement

In the framework of benefit-cost analysis, benefits refer to those results or outcomes of an intervention that can be assessed in monetary terms. The foundation of benefit-cost analysis were constructed in the evaluation of water resource projects (Eckstein, 1958). It was found that most of the outcomes of such projects could be measured in terms of their monetary values. For example, hydroelectric dams produce electricity, potable water, and flood control. The benefits of the electricity and potable water can be determined by applying the appropriate prices of those outputs to the amounts that are produced. The benefits of flood control can be computed by ascertaining the amount of property that would have been lost in the absence of the construction of the dam. Usually this is determined from historical data on the extent of flooding that took place as well as the value of property that would have been lost if similar floods were to take place in the future.

When these are added together one is able to derive an estimate of the monetary value of benefits of a hydroelectric dam. These can be compared with the costs of the dam to see if the benefits exceed the costs. Further, the benefits and costs can be compared with those of other projects to see which have the lowest CB ratios or the greatest excess of benefits over costs. Not only can different water resource projects be compared with each other to see which are the best social investments, but they can also be compared with any social project for which cost and benefit data are available. Thus one could compare health projects with transportation and educational projects to see which should be undertaken by society.

Of course, even for many of these areas, it is not always possible to find appropriate ways to express the benefits of a project in monetary terms. While the electricity and potable water production and flood control can be readily converted into their monetary values, this is less true of the recreational and aesthetic aspects of different water resource projects. There are no fully acceptable methods of determining the monetary value to society of these less tangible benefits, that is, the value of a beautiful vista or of a recreational experience. However, it is believed that the major outcomes of such projects can be valued in monetary terms, and adjustments can be made in the calculations for taking account of incommensurables or those outcomes whose translation into monetary measures is problematic.

Areas of Potential for
Cost-Benefit Studies

In the case of education, the types of results that may lend themselves to cost-benefit analysis are especially those relating to labor market outcomes of education (Becker, 1964; Ribich, 1968; Weisbrod, 1965). For example, vocational education is designed to train persons for immediate employment upon completion of secondary school (Hu and Stromsdorfer, 1979). In order to see if vocational education is a good investment, it is possible to do a cost-benefit analysis in which the benefits refer to the earnings of graduates. In this way, cost-benefit comparisons can be made of vocational programs in different specialties as well as between vocational and general training programs for high school graduates. For each group it is possible to determine both the costs of the training program and the monetary value of the earnings of graduates. Clearly, programs that are able to obtain placements for their graduates with steady employment and high earnings will show higher benefits than those with poorer employment and earnings records.

School districts and state educational agencies might wish to determine which vocational educational curricula have the lowest cost-benefit ratios and whether vocational education has a lower CB ratio than general education. On the basis of this information it is possible to reallocate resources in those directions that will maximize the employment and earnings potential of graduates of the programs. That is, programs with CB ratios greater than one — meaning that costs exceed benefits — would be phased out in favor of those with the lowest CB ratios. In these cases the results of vocational educational programs would be assessed only according to the value of earnings that they generated for graduates. That is, if there were some other redeeming aspect of such programs, it would not be accounted for by this methodology. However, given the purpose of vocational education to enhance the vocational success of youth, this omission may not be of serious concern.

In general, the way to use CB analysis in education is to address the increase in earnings of enrollees as the measure of benefits of programs. An investment in education or training results in higher earnings for the trainee relative to similar persons who did not benefit from this investment. Since these additional earnings will accrue to the individual for each year of work following the program completion, we need to estimate the benefits in terms of their present value. That is, we wish to look at the present value of the benefits to compare them with the present value of the costs. Both benefits and costs occur over a number of years, so the cost-benefit comparison will mean comparing the present values of both at the time that the investment is initiated. The techniques for doing this are well-established in the literature (e.g., Becker, 1964; Cohn, 1979, Chaps. 5-6), so the reader is advised to review those sources for details.

Thus programs that attempt to reduce the number of high school dropouts could compare the costs of those programs with the benefits in terms of increased earnings of persons who are saved from dropping out (Weisbrod, 1965). CB calculations can also be made to see if it is worthwhile for an individual or for a population to undertake additional schooling, and the CB estimates can be made for different types of education. Further, CB analysis is an appropriate way of assessing the value of social investments in training programs for the unemployed or underemployed and choosing among them with regard to areas of training.

Challenges to Cost-Benefit Analysis

Even when it is appropriate to assess the results of an educational intervention through its effects on earnings of participants, the measurement of earnings is often problematic. Consider that while the education or training program that is the subject of the evaluation can be reviewed at the present to ascertain its costs, the effects of the program on the earnings of the participants can be known only in the future. This creates two major problems for determining the benefits of the program. The first is the question of the time period following the program over which earnings must be observed, and the second is the issue of a comparison of earnings patterns with those of similar persons who did not receive the benefits of the education or training program.

Since the effects of the program should be visited on the earnings of the participants over their working lives, there are obvious problems in making a timely evaluation unless one is able to make accurate projections from the earnings information received in a relatively short period following the training. However, earnings immediately following the education or training might not be representative of differences over a lifetime. For example, the earnings effects of the program may be overstated if the program is able to provide better jobs and higher levels of employment for its graduates on the basis of placement effort rather than skill development. In the longer run, persons without the training who did not have the advantages of such placement services may catch up in earnings. In the short run, however, this will not be observed. The opposite bias occurs when there is a tendency to understate the earnings effects of the program because those who received the training increase their earnings advantages over time more than did those without training. Again, a short period of observation of earnings will not reflect these trends.

Further, one must compare the earnings performances of participants with a control group of similar persons who did not undertake the training or education. This requirement imposes additional burdens on the evaluation in terms of selecting an appropriate control group or providing statistical controls on other factors that could affect earnings. There is also the difficulty of doing a longitudinal evaluation of differences in earnings patterns. Both the problems of having to observe earnings after the educational intervention and having to obtain a control group for a proper earnings comparison set out difficult requirements in terms of evaluation costs and time. One cannot get quick evaluations of such programs in order to implement those that are most successful, and the costs of the evaluations will be relatively high.

For these reasons, CB evaluations often take a variety of shortcuts, such as observing labor market and earnings experiences for only short periods after training; utilizing comparison groups that are chosen on the basis of data availability or convenience, rather than precise compatibility; or using earnings data from general sources such as the U.S. Bureau of the

Census to approximate the earnings differences among persons with different levels of education. For example, the estimated earnings of a particular population after receiving some additional level of education are often assumed to be identical to those of groups with characteristics similar to those of the trainees, where data on the latter are taken from the census or other general sources (Hanoch, 1967). Essentially, statistical controls are used instead of a control group. Further, the present lifetime earnings patterns may not be an accurate benchmark for estimating future ones (Eckaus, 1973). To a large degree the researcher must use these approaches because of the lack of good alternatives.

In summary, the use of CB analysis in education is most appropriate when educational and training outcomes can be evaluated in terms of the additional earnings generated among participants by their training or education. Even an evaluation of these benefits, however, requires a study design that must allow for a considerable time period to obtain earnings data and substantial resources to enable the collection and analysis of the information. Even the best of the CB studies in education must make some compromises in their design because of the difficulties of assessing educationally created differences in lifetime incomes. These restrictions mean that for most educational evaluations the CB framework will be less appropriate than cost-effectiveness or cost-utility. The restrictions imposed on the measurement of benefits and the time and other resources required to do such analyses will often preclude consideration of CB approaches. The general issues can be reviewed in Stokey and Zeckhauser (1978, Chaps. 9-10) and Mishan (1976).

Effectiveness and Its Measurement

The use of the cost-effectiveness approach frees the evaluator from many of these requirements by enabling a more direct measure of impact in terms of the effectiveness of the intervention on a specific outcome. This outcome can be addressed according to its own attributes, rather than having to convert it into monetary units. Thus student learning can be assessed in terms of test scores; dropout prevention programs can be evaluated according to the numbers of potential dropouts who complete programs; physical education programs can be viewed in terms of the improvement in various physical skills of participants; and so on. The CE approach, then, permits a straightforward evaluation of alternative programs that have the same objectives. Obviously, programs with different objectives will have different indicators of effectiveness, so they cannot be readily compared within the CE framework. The CE approach is appropriate, however, as long as the problem is that of attempting to choose from among competing alternatives for accomplishing a similar goal.

The CE approach has a number of very important advantages, relative to CB analysis, that recommend it for educational evaluations. First, the measures of educational effectiveness can be those which a decision maker will normally consider, such as improvements in students' test scores and other student proficiencies. Different measures of effectiveness can be tailored for different goals, and the units of measurement can be those which are familiar to educational decision makers. Second, the CE approach builds on rather standard approaches to evaluation, simply adding a cost dimension to the overall evaluation design. Thus, if evaluations of effectiveness among different alternatives will be undertaken in any event, it is necessary only to provide a framework for incorporating the cost analysis into the evaluation. Finally, CE evaluations will generally require less time and other resources than CB studies, because assessments of effectiveness can be done during the operation or at the termination of the programs that are being evaluated. In contrast, CB studies with their reliance on increased earnings of participants must usually rely on longitudinal follow-ups of the participants well after the completion of the education or training programs that are being evaluated.

Effectiveness Measures

CE represents a more suitable framework for doing most types of educational evaluations than does CB. The richness in potential of the CE approach is reflected in Table 6.1, which provides examples of how effectiveness might be assessed. Almost any particular program objective can be utilized as a basis for constructing an effectiveness measure. This table shows a number of examples of different program objectives — from reducing dropouts to student learning to student satisfaction to placements in college and in jobs. The CE approach can be used to evaluate a very wide variety of program types.

In order to use the CE approach, it is first necessary to determine the program objective and an appropriate measure of effectiveness. Then the alternatives that will be evaluated must be specified. Given these requirements, it is possible to design an evaluation of the alternatives on the particular criterion of effectiveness that has been established and to obtain cost information for each alternative. Finally, the cost and effectiveness data can be combined into CE ratios that show the amount of effectiveness that can be obtained for an estimated cost. Since these ratios can be compared among alternatives, it is possible to provide information to decision makers on which alternatives seem to be most parsimonious in terms of costs,

TABLE 6.1   Examples of Effectiveness Measures

Program Objective	Measure of Effectiveness
Program completions	Number of students completing program
Reducing dropouts	Number of potential dropouts who graduate
Employment of graduates	Number of graduates placed in appropriate jobs
Student learning	Test scores in appropriate domains utilizing appropriate test instruments
Student satisfaction	Student assessment of program on appropriate instrument to measure satisfaction
Physical performance	Evaluation of student physical condition and physical skills
College placement	Number of students placed in colleges of particular types
Advance college placement	Number of courses and units received by students in advance placement, by subject

with respect to the measure of effectiveness that is under scrutiny.

In summary, the CE approach is a rather natural one for educational evaluations, because it lends itself readily to the traditional evaluation approaches and to the types of outcomes that are often considered by decision makers. However, even the CE approach requires a substantial investment in terms of an evaluation design and activity to obtain measures of effectiveness. Evaluations of curriculum or teacher characteristics on student achievement may require (1) substantial testing programs both before and after the interventions; (2) major data collection and analysis activities; and (3) a significant period of time to plan and conduct the study and to evaluate outcomes. For example, it is not unreasonable to require at least a two-year period for a one-year study of educational interventions that are designed to alter student achievement. Time is needed prior to the initiation of the evaluation to plan it and to marshal the logistical resources that are required, and time is needed after the data are collected to analyze the results. In many cases, however, it is important to have data on costs and probable results within a considerably shorter time frame. In that case, the CU approach is probably more appropriate.

Cost-Utility:
Concept and Measurement

A major advantage of both CE and CB analyses is that each approach can be applied according to an explicit set of premises and procedures that can be replicated by others. The reason for this is that each is based upon a set of explicit assumptions and relations, which can be modified if they seem inappropriate. A disadvantage is that these procedures and the information requirements that underlie them require considerable time and evaluation resources to implement. Often the decision maker lacks the luxury of time and other resources to carry out an evaluation. As a rule of thumb, even a simple CE or CB evaluation is likely to take six months. Of course, that investment in time, personnel, and other resources may be well worthwhile, because it may save many times its cost in terms of the value of the information that it provides. As a practical matter, however, many decisions must be made on the basis of studies that must be completed in weeks rather than months or years. In that case, it is still possible to provide a systematic approach that incorporates costs by doing a cost-utility evaluation.

The advantage of CU analysis is its flexibility with respect to evaluating a wide range of alternatives in a short period of time with few information requirements and restrictions regarding the measurement of outcomes. The disadvantages are that the technique relies upon a much higher degree of subjective judgment than do the other approaches — judgments that cannot be made explicit since they are really opinions (albeit informed opinions). In essence, CU analysis compares the subjective values or utilities that are placed on each alternative by an appropriate audience with the costs of that alternative. Alternatives are then compared to see which provide the highest utility relative to cost. These alternatives are said to have the lowest CU ratios.

There is one important restriction that we should apply to CU analysis. Its results should never be recommended to a secondary audience, since its procedures are permeated with the subjective judgments of the primary audiences and constituencies. Since such judgments cannot be considered to be replicable among different audiences, the CU results should be viewed as unique to a particular setting rather than as being of use to some other setting.

The Nature
and Use of Utility

What is meant by "utility"? This term refers to an attempt to measure the degree of happiness created by an activity. The concept dates to the early nineteenth century, when a group of British philosophers known as the Philharmonic Radicals attempted to construct a theory of society in which activities would be arranged to provide the greatest happiness to the greatest number of people (Halevy, 1955). The approach was known as utilitarianism — a term coined by its principal spokesman, Jeremy Bentham — because every social institution was to be evaluated for its utility in providing social happiness. Thus the notion of cost-utility refers to attempting to ascertain the value, usefulness, or contribution to social happiness of a particular activity relative to the cost of providing that activity.

Since happiness is exceedingly difficult to measure, the analyst assesses the utility of an alternative by asking the respondent to rate it on a measurement scale. Thus the measurement of utility represents an attempt to obtain numerical valuations of utility of different respondents, and these are aggregated to provide an overall utility rating for each alternative. Alternatives can then be compared on the basis of their estimated value or utility and their costs. This can best be understood through an example.

——— Example: Cost-Utility Analysis and Budget Cuts ———

In recent years both the federal and state governments are experiencing pressures to reduce or constrain government spending. When combined with the impact of declining enrollments, local educational agencies have faced financial hardships and have had to search for ways to reduce expenditures. A given school district finds that it will have a shortfall in revenues of $200,000 for the next fiscal year. The school board asks the administration to provide a recommended set of cuts and their justification within the next six weeks. The administration decides that it would like to use a cost-utility analysis to select among alternatives in such a way that the impact of the cuts on the educational program of the district is minimized. Accordingly, the following steps are pursued.

First, the educational programs and services of the school district are divided between those that are discretionary and those that are mandatory. Mandatory programs are those required by the state or existing federal funding sources, or by the district for meeting graduation requirements and other standards. The discretionary programs are described briefly in terms of their objectives, the numbers of students who are served, and any evidence on the performance of such programs (e.g., test scores or advanced-placement successes or number of transitions made from bilingual instruction to regular instruction). Based upon these brief descriptions, parents are asked to rank each program on a scale of 0 to

10, in which 10 reflects the highest priority and 0 the lowest priority. The results are tallied to ascertain the average utility rating for each program.

At the same time, the ingredients method is used to ascertain the ingredients that it would be saved by cutting the program. These are converted into marginal costs savings for each program by valuing the ingredients according to their costs. In this case the ingredients for each program are divided between those that could be relinquished and those that must be retained because of tenure contracts or other fixed obligations. That is, there is no cost saving for ingredients that must be kept even if they are not used. Finally, the costs are distributed among constituencies, so that the school district reviews only its cost in the analysis that follows.

Each program is then ranked according to its marginal cost to the school district and according to its utility, in that the one with the lowest CU ratio is placed at the bottom of the list and that with the highest CU ratio is placed at the top of the list. This means that activities at the top of the list have a higher cost relative to their estimated value than those at the bottom of the list. Beginning at the top of the list, activities are nominated for cuts until a total of $200,000 in cuts is obtained. This list of cuts is recommended to the school board with a description of the procedures that were followed and a complete list of the CU ratios for all of the alternatives.

In short, the procedure begins with the normal identification of the problem and the specification of alternatives. Next, however, an appropriate audience is selected to rate the alternatives according to the criteria set out for the decision and accurate descriptive information on each alternative. These ratings or utilities are summed and divided by the number of ratings to obtain average utilities for each program. Cost data are collected independent of the ratings. When the utilities and costs are integrated into CU ratios, the decision maker attempts to retain or expand programs with low CU ratios and reduce or eliminate ones with high CU ratios. The overall objective is to select those alternatives that will provide the highest level of utility or satisfaction for any total cost constraint.

Two major questions that are raised are the following:

— Who should rate the utility of alternatives?

— What is the validity of adding up the separate ratings of different respondents to obtain an overall utility rating for each alternative?

In general, the persons who rate alternatives should be those persons who will be affected by them — that is, the stakeholders (Byrk, 1983). The value of any set of alternatives can best be judged by an informed clientele who will experience the consequences of the alternatives that are chosen. Thus a representative sample of students and parents might be appropriate for assessing the value of different educational programs. In some cases, however, it will not be possible to obtain the views of a large sample of clientele in the community or schools because of a time or other constraint. In that particular case one would wish to obtain the views of appropriate representatives of the clientele, such as school board members or elected officials of civic and community organizations or student organizations.

In other cases it may be possible for the administrators and decision makers themselves to determine the utility scores of the alternatives. For example, if we take the case of a situation in which the overall goals of an educational entity are clear, it may be possible to estimate the utilities of the alternatives with respect to their contributions in reaching these goals. That is, the decision makers may wish to gather all of the available information on each alternative and rate the alternatives with regard to their value to the school or school district in meeting the objectives that have been set out by the school board or parents.

The question of how the utility scores of individual respondents can be combined to obtain an overall utility score for each alternative is somewhat more troublesome. A great deal of analytic thought has been devoted to the meaning of utility scales and their usefulness (Fishburn, 1964). Of particular concern are a number of "weak" properties. First, such scales can be thought to have only ordinal, rather than cardinal, meaning. By this is meant that the differences in utility values assigned by a respondent can designate only an ordering of utility in that a higher value implies greater utility than a lower value. The scales do not normally have interval properties in the sense that a score of 8 denotes twice as much utility as a score of 4. Clearly, we hope that there is some relation between the score and the amount of utility, but it cannot be demonstrated that the scales have interval properties in any strong sense. The attempt to approach cardinality in measurement can be enhanced by stressing to the respondent that he or she should treat the scale as if it has interval properties. This can be done by explaining in layperson's terms the characteristics of the scale and the way in which the respondent should use it to rate programs.

A second problem is that we cannot assume that the same value on a utility scale has the same meaning to different raters. Some individuals will tend to rate even their lowest priorities with high values, while others will tend to rate even their highest priorities with low values. In a sense, this subjective process is inspired by different explicit reference points for what is high and what is low. Thus an interpersonal comparison of scores is risky, and one just hopes that the vagaries of individual reference points is a random phenomenon among individuals and will not be reflected in the aggregate scores when the overall score among respondents is computed. This problem can also be partially alleviated by instructing the respondent on the meaning of different parts of the scale. For example, a utility scale of 0-10 might have guidelines next to each value so that 0 denotes no contribution, 5 denotes an average contribution, and 10 denotes the highest possible contribution.

This brings us to the main issue: the appropriate method for combining individual scores. While adding the individual utility scores of respondents may seem to be logically valid, it requires a number of strong assumptions to assume that such a method is appropriate. First, one must assume that the scales approach the ideal of interval measurement in order for the summation procedure to have meaning. Second, one must assume that the "grand" utility score is a sum of the individual scores, so that one need only add the utilities of individuals to get the total score. Yet, if there are interactions among individuals such that the scores should really be multiplied or combined in some other way to get a "socially" valid utility measure, the summation procedure will not be appropriate (Arrow, 1963). There are other issues of utility measurement and aggregation that will not be addressed here, but it will suffice to say that it has a shakier conceptual basis than we would like for a tool that is logically so compelling and so easy to apply. On the positive side, there is no a priori bias in its use; it is easily and readily implementable; and as a pragmatic matter it has very attractive properties. Following is an example of how school administrators might use cost-utility analysis to choose among alternatives. The reader should also refer to other sources and approaches to the practice of cost-utility, such as Edwards and Newman (1982), Keeney and Raiffa (1976), and Stokey and Zeckhauser (1978, Chap. 12).

─────── **Example: Rating Alternative Reading Programs** ───────

Assume that the school board decides that reading is a high priority for the next year. The school administration is asked to select new curricula and teacher-training approaches to improve the teaching of reading. Different curricula and teacher-training approaches are sought by the administration from both commercial publishers and other sources. For each alternative, the administration requests information on the nature of the curriculum, its strategy, and evidence on its success. In addition, the cost implications of each are estimated through the standard ingredients approach.

At this stage all of the teachers, curriculum specialists, and relevant administrators are asked to rate the alternatives in the following way. Each alternative is described in terms of the basic strategy that is embodied, the materials and training that are required, and the evidence on its success for different groups of children. On the basis of this information, each respondent is asked to rate the value or utility of each alternative on the following four dimensions: increasing reading speed, increasing reading comprehension, increasing word knowledge, and increasing student satisfaction with reading. The utilities for each alternative are averaged across respondents for each of the four dimensions of rating. The result is that each alternative will have four utility scores, one for each dimension of performance.

The utility rating for each dimension and the cost for each alternative will be used to create CU ratios. On this basis there will be four rankings of the alternatives, one for each performance dimension. If the ratings are relatively consistent among dimensions, administrators will select from those alternatives with the lowest CU ratios to establish new curriculum and teacher-training approaches to improve reading. Of course, even the present method of teaching reading can be included as an alternative that should be rated and evaluated. If the ratings of alternatives are not highly consistent along the performance dimensions, it will be necessary to derive some average of the ratings of utility to create the CU ratios that will be used for decision making. One possibility is to weigh each of the dimensions equally in setting the overall utility ratings for the four dimensions of performance. Another is to obtain utility weights for the performance dimensions themselves to determine how heavily to count each dimension in the overall utility rating for each alternative.

Table 6.2 represents this situation by showing the utility ratings and CU ratios of alternatives for improving reading. Five alternative approaches are selected for evaluation by the administration. The additional costs or marginal costs for each approach are computed on a per-student basis. Information on all of the alternatives is circulated to a panel of teachers, principals, curriculum specialists, and other administrators, and each respondent is asked to rate the utility value of each alternative in meeting each of the four performance goals for reading: speed, comprehension, word knowledge, and student satisfaction. The utility scale has a range of 0-10, the bottom of the scale denotes no value in expectations of reaching the goal, and the top of the scale denotes the maximum value in expectations of reaching the goal. The utility scores listed for each alternative and performance dimension represent the arithmetic means of the responses. Respondents are also asked to provide a utility rating for each goal on a similar 0-10-point scale, in which the importance of each goal is rated. These scores are shown at the bottom of the table under the performance-dimensions columns.

The total utility score for each alternative represents a summation of the utility ratings across the four dimensions. The average weighted score represents an attempt to weigh the score for each performance dimension by the importance of that dimension as reflected in the utility values assigned to that dimension by the respondents. In a more mechanical sense, the average weighted score is determined by multiplying for each performance dimension the utility rating for that dimension times the utility score on that dimension for each alternative, summing the four products of this exercise for each alternative, and dividing by four to obtain an average weighted score for each alternative.

TABLE 6.2 Utility Ratings and CU Ratios of Alternatives for Improving Reading

| Alternative | Cost per Student | Performance Dimensions[1] | | | | Utility Scores | | CU Ratios | |
		S	C	WK	Sat.	Total Score[2]	Average Weighted Score[3]	Total Score[4]	Weighted Score[5]
A	$56	8	6	6	7	27	50.50	2.07	1.11
B	51	5	4	6	3	18	34.00	2.83	1.50
C	70	6	9	7	7	29	55.00	2.41	1.27
D	65	4	9	9	5	27	51.50	2.41	1.26
E	93	9	6	4	6	24	47.50	3.88	1.96
Utility Weights for Each Performance		8	9	7	6				

1. Performance dimensions: S = speed; C = comprehension; WK = word knowledge; Sat. = Student Satisfaction.
2. Total score is the sum of the utility ratings for the four performance dimensions.
3. Average Weighted Score is determined by multiplying for each performance dimension the utility rating for that dimension times the utility score on that dimenstion for each alternative, summing the four products of this exercise, and dividing by four to obtain an average weighted score.
4. CU Total Score is derived by dividing the Cost per Student by the Total Score.
5. CU Weighted Score is obtained by dividing the Cost per Student by the Weighted Score.

The final columns of the table show the CU ratios that were derived by dividing the cost per student by the appropriate utility scores. The lowest CU ratios imply the lowest cost for a given level of utility, and the highest CU ratios imply the highest cost. On this basis, alternative A appears to be the most preferable one as evidenced by the lowest CU ratio, and alternative E appears to be the least preferable one because of its very high cost relative to its utility scores. Alternatives C and D appear to be about equal in terms of CU ratings, and alternative B is next to the bottom in terms of CU attractiveness. These results should always be tempered by a discussion of their meaning and an exploration of factors (such as ease of implementation) that may not have been included in the analysis, before choosing an alternative. That is, the CU findings ought to enter the discussion prominently, but the choice should not be mechanically based on the CU ratings without considering other pertinent factors. If choices are made that are at odds with the CU recommendations, the reasons for not accepting the CU priorities ought to be explicit.

Treatment of Multiple Outcomes

One of the challenges implicit in many evaluations is how to treat a situation in which there is more than one outcome of the intervention or set of alternatives. For example, a curriculum, teacher-training, or educational-technology intervention may affect several measures of achievement, including reading and arithmetic proficiencies, analytic performance, and general knowledge. Depending upon the particular alternative, the results on all of these dimensions may differ in ways that mean that the best or most cost-effective alternative for one outcome is a poor choice if one emphasizes a different outcome. Thus the problem of multiple outcomes is to ascertain how one can set criteria to make cost-effective choices that take account of all of the important outcomes.

This dilemma can be seen more clearly if one considers the single outcome case. Assume that all of the alternatives affect only a single objective: increasing reading scores. In this case there is a single index of performance or effectiveness, which can be combined with costs to create a criterion for decision making. Now assume that different alternatives have different impacts on the components of reading scores. Those which have the largest effect on increasing comprehension have the smallest effect on increasing speed and word knowledge.

Table 6.3 presents some hypothetical scores on examinations for three domains related to reading performance for three different alternative reading programs. Assume that these are standard scores, such as percentile ranks, so that the performance metric is similar for each dimension of outcome. This is an important criterion for the multiple outcome case — that the outcome measures be assessed according to a similar scale. The reason for this is that when we later multiply them by their utility values, we do not want the product of that calculation to be influenced by different measurement scales among the outcomes.

According to Table 6.3, both comprehension and word knowledge are higher among alternatives in which reading speed is lower and vice versa. That means that there may be some trade-offs in seeking to apply approaches that increase reading speed. The question that arises is how this information might be combined with costs to obtain an overall criterion for decision making.

Obviously, if only one outcome — reading speed — is used for a cost-effectiveness analysis, the CE results will differ from those that would be obtained by using a different outcome — comprehension. Thus, one must reject the use of any single dimension for making a CE determination. The principal solution is to convert this CE approach into a CU approach by rating the importance of each outcome on a utility scale. For example, a panel of reading experts could be asked to weigh the importance of each dimension on a utility scale of 0 to 10. The respondent might first be asked to set priorities in terms of

TABLE 6.3 Multiple Outcomes of Alternative Reading Programs

Alternative	Speed	Comprehension	Word Knowledge
A	75	40	55
B	60	65	65
C	85	30	35

which outcome seems most important, second-most important, and least important in terms of overall reading skills and usefulness. The second question could ask the respondent to be more precise by indicating that importance on a utility scale.

Assume that the experts set a utility value of 7 for speed, 9 for comprehension, and 6 for word knowledge. If we multiply each of these utility weights by the appropriate scores and provide a summation of them for each alternative, we are able to obtain Table 6.4. These utility scores can then be combined with cost data to obtain CU ratios. In this way, any multiple-outcome problem can be converted from a cost-effectiveness approach to a cost-utility approach in order to incorporate all of the outcomes into the analysis. Of course, this problem does not arise in CB analysis, because all of the outcomes are already converted into a common measure of outcome — monetary values.

Distribution of Benefits and Effects

As with the distribution of costs among those bearing the burden, it is important to consider which constituencies receive the benefits or share in the effects of each alternative. In some cases the distributional consequences do not vary among recipients, but in others they do. For example, one might be concerned with the types of students that educational interventions assist the most. A specific alternative may increase total test scores by having profound effects on those with the highest initial score and little or no effect on those with the lowest initial scores. Alternatively, an intervention might have stronger ef-

TABLE 6.4 Utility Ratings of Outcomes of Reading Programs

Alternative	Speed	Comprehension	Word Knowledge	Total Utility Score
A	525	360	330	1215
B	420	585	390	1395
C	595	270	210	1075

fects for those with low scores initially or might have equal effects for all groups. Likewise, there can be different distributional consequences among the races and income groups, and between genders. Not only is this an important issue to review in evaluations generally, but it also ought to be taken into account when incorporating costs into the analysis.

Essentially, this problem is really a variant of the multiple-outcome one. Any overall result can be decomposed among the populations that are affected to see how each shares in the outcome. Then utility values can be used to weight the results according to social priorities. Thus interventions to increase the educational performance of disadvantaged youngsters might be given a utility value of 10, while gains for the more advantaged might be given lower values in considering alternatives to help the disadvantaged (Ribich, 1968, Chap. 2; Weisbrod, 1968). By converting the distributional issues to a multiple-outcome case, the same techniques as were used above can be used to assess the value of the total result.

Summary

This chapter reviewed various aspects of benefits, effectiveness, and utility to show how they might be formulated, measured, and combined with costs. Each of these areas has its own literature, which should be pursued for further details. The primary purpose of this chapter was to provide an understanding of how the cost analyses developed in earlier chapters could be combined with the analyses of results of educational interventions. The final chapter of this primer addresses the uses and abuses of cost analysis.

Exercises

1. What types of educational interventions lend themselves best to CB analyses? Why?

2. Three years ago a community college district considered the establishment of a number of new vocational curricula. A special committee was

appointed by the college trustees. The committee was composed of local businessmen and taxpayers as well as students, faculty, and administrators. The committee reviewed various employment surveys and interviewed area employers. Based upon these activities it recommended twelve new programs for the college district. The college followed this advice, only to find that some of the programs were experiencing low enrollments and relatively poor placements. After three years the district has asked you to do a cost-benefit analysis of the programs to see which should be continued and which should be phased out. Design a study that would meet those objectives. What are the benefits and what are the costs? How would you measure them? How should your results be used to make a decision?

3. Select an evaluation with which you are familiar. Describe the problem that was addressed and the alternatives that were considered. What measures of effectiveness were used and why? How would you do a study of costs to convert the evaluation into a cost-effectiveness analysis?

4. In the evaluation that you reviewed in the previous exercise, can you think of other dimensions of effectiveness that might have been considered? How would you add these dimensions to the overall design?

5. A school district is concerned about its shortages of mathematics and science teachers. An advisory group suggests the following alternative solutions to the problem.

(a) Pay salary differentials to attract more mathematics and science teachers.

(b) Ask local industry to contribute teaching time from among their scientists and mathematicians.

(c) Use computer-assisted instruction and video-cassettes, in conjunction with college mathematics and science students, to offer instruction.

You are asked to design a cost analysis that can evaluate these alternatives and select the one that will be most preferable for the district.

6. What are some of the advantages and disadvantages of CU in comparison with CB and CE analyses?

7. What is meant by "utility," and what are some of the problems in measuring it?

8. A high school offers two years of each of the following languages: French, German, Russian, and Spanish. It wishes to offer four more years of language instruction by adding one or two more years of instruction for each of these languages and/or by offering up to two years of Latin. Design a CU analysis that will assist the high school administration in choosing the best combination of languages in which to offer additional instruction.

9. Different educational alternatives have different educational results among different student groups (e.g., disadvantaged versus advantaged, Hispanic versus Anglo, males versus females). How can CU analysis be used to consider these distributional effects as well as the overall educational results of each alternative?

CHAPTER **7**

The Use of Cost Evaluations

OBJECTIVES

1. *Demonstrate how to use the results of cost evaluations.*
2. *Discuss how to use reports based upon cost evaluations.*
3. *Present suggestions for implementing cost analysis in evaluation.*

THE PREVIOUS CHAPTERS explained the importance of using cost analysis in evaluations as well as the different modes of analysis within the cost family. In addition, attention was devoted to identifying the problem, specifying alternatives, and choosing an appropriate cost-analysis approach. Following these introductory issues, chapters were devoted to the identification, measurement, and distribution of costs as well as the measurement of benefits, effects, and utility. In this chapter I wish to focus on the uses and abuses of cost analysis and, particularly, on the utilization of results of such studies for decision making.

Use of Results

I have argued that when cost-effectiveness analysis and other cost analyses are integrated into evaluations, the evaluation exercise is more likely to yield the types of information that are crucial to decisions than when costs are ignored. This does not mean that even the best CB, CE, or CU studies can be used mechanically to make decisions. The purpose of this section is to explain how the results of these studies might be used productively in the decision-making context.

Perhaps the most important principle is that of viewing such studies as sources of information rather than as sources of decisions. Any analytic or evaluative tool can only provide information to inform decisions. There are a number of reasons that even the best analyses must be combined with other types of information in order to make good decisions. The fundamental problem is that as helpful as evaluation studies can be in providing information on alternatives, they must necessarily be incomplete.

First, even if they are very well conceived and implemented, both measures of costs and of benefits, effects, and utilities are really *estimates* of those dimensions. This does not mean that they are biased or misleading, but they are always subject to some error. Their accuracy will depend heavily upon the integration of the cost or effectiveness concept that is sought and the ability to measure it in an accurate way. Even the best procedures will have some margin for error, which must be considered in terms of the magnitude of the disparities. When the differences in CB, CE, and CU ratings among alternatives are large, the results should be taken more seriously than when differences are small. Small differences might be accounted for by measurement errors alone.

Second, it is never possible to incorporate all of the considerations into an evaluation that should inform the final decision. All evaluations reduce complex organizational and social dynamics to a manageable set of relations for analysis. While every effort should be made to consider the principal issues, there may be other factors that can be taken into account only as one reviews the results of cost evaluations. For example, there may exist institutional or organizational factors that make one alternative easier to implement than another. Implementation of a new intervention is hardly a mechanical task, and many alternatives that show promise at the drawing-board stage are relegated to failure at the implementation stage because of the simplistic assumptions underlying them (Berman & McLaughlin, 1975). Those alternatives that are presently being used or that are similar to present approaches are more likely to provide the predicted results than those that represent a radical departure from existing practices. Clearly, this information must be taken into account in considering the implications of cost evaluations. For example, if one alternative seems slightly more cost-effective than another but will require massive changes in organizational structure, it may be appropriate to select the slightly less cost-effective approach that is more easily implementable.

The important point is that there are always considerations that cannot be fully incorporated into the evaluations. At the decision stage, however, these considerations should be explicated and brought into play in using the information generated by the cost evaluations. There are two general implications that flow from these concerns. First, small differences in CB, CE, and CU results should never be taken seriously. When the results are relatively similar for two or more alternatives, the decision should be made on the basis of other criteria rather than on comparisons of numbers in the third decimal place. As a general rule, differences of ten percent or so in CB, CE, and CU ratios should always be treated with skepticism. Differences of this magnitude can easily be attributable to conventional margins of error.

In contrast, differences of 100 percent or more in CB, CE, or CU ratios between or among alternatives ought to be taken very seriously. First, one must ask why the differences are so substantial. If the answer to this question does not provide any basis for skepticism, the results should be used to inform the ultimate decision. In every case it is important to consider the magnitude of the differences and what types of considerations were not included in the analysis before choosing an alternative. The decision maker should never use the results of such analyses in a mechanical fashion, such that the decision is simply a lockstep extension of the results. Rather, the results provide information (albeit extremely important information) that must be combined with other pertinent data in selecting alternatives.

Example: Making Decisions with Cost-Effectiveness Findings

The constituents of a certain school district are deeply concerned about the problem of dropouts at the secondary level. After interviewing former students who dropped out, it is concluded that the main reasons contributing to dropping out are poor academic performance, boredom, and pregnancies among female students. Accordingly, three alternative programs are formulated to reduce dropouts. All three programs provide greater information on birth control and responsible sexual behavior in order to reduce pregnancies. In addition, alternative A concentrates on upgrading the academic skills of dropouts by instituting a program of token rewards in which students obtain scrip for good behavior and performance. When enough scrip is obtained, it can be exchanged for merchandise. Alternative B focuses on additional academic assistance through peer tutoring as well as placement in part-time jobs for those students who desire them. Alternative C focuses on an intensive counseling program incorporating group and individual counseling methods to address both academic and nonacademic problems of students.

On the basis of evaluations of former dropouts, the school district concludes that the following students are dropout-prone: those with test scores in the bottom 30 percent of the population; those who have been characterized by disruptive behavior; and those with poor attendance records and, especially, unexcused absences. Any one of these characteristics or any combination of these seems to provide an early warning of dropout-proneness on the basis of past records. The school district randomly assigns 300 tenth-grade students who are characterized as dropout-prone into four groups of 75. The first group is a control group that will not receive any special treatment. Each of the other three groups will be the focus of one of the three program interventions to reduce dropouts. On the basis of a one-year intervention, data are collected on dropouts for all four groups. The control group has the highest proportion of dropouts, as expected, and each of the treatment groups has fewer dropouts. The difference between the number of students who dropped out and the number who were expected to drop out, as reflected in the experience of the control group, is used to assess the effects of each program in reducing dropouts.

Table 7.1 shows the cost for reducing dropouts for the three alternative programs. Of the 75 students in the control group, 35 had dropped out by the end of the year. Among the other groups, there were fewer dropouts, suggesting that each had prevented some dropout-prone youngsters from leaving. Using the control group as a basis for estimating the number of dropouts in the absence of program interventions, it appears that 17 students were saved from dropping out by Program A; 15 students were saved by Program B; and 10 students were prevented from dropping out by Program C. Total costs for each program were fairly similar, but the "cost per prevented dropout" showed that Program C was the most costly, while Programs A and B were rather close in costs per prevented dropout.

Because Programs A and B were so close in the cost per prevented dropout, other information was sought to inform the decision. One of the crucial factors determining the implementation of a program is that of teacher attitudes. Accordingly, a survey was made of teacher attitudes toward the three alternatives. First, teachers were given a

TABLE 7.1   Cost for Reducing Dropouts for Three Alternative Programs

Alternative	Total Cost	Number of Dropouts	Dropouts Prevented	Cost per Prevented Dropout	Teacher Attitudes
A	$12,750	18	17	$ 750	resistant
B	12,375	20	15	825	enthusiastic
C	13,500	25	10	1,350	neutral
Control Group	—	35	—	—	—

description of each program and what would be required in terms of teacher participation. Second, they were asked to rank the programs according to their own preferences, and to give the reasons for those preferences. Third, they were asked to provide any information that they thought ought to be considered by the administration in making a program decision. On the basis of this survey it was concluded that teachers would be resistant to the adoption of Program A; enthusiastic about Program B; and neutral about Program C.

When this information was combined with the cost per prevented dropout, the decision makers concluded that Program B should be implemented. Although Program A was less costly for each success in its experimental setting, a higher risk was attached to its full implementation by the apparent resistance of teachers to the program of token rewards. Since the teachers were enthusiastic about Program B, it was assumed that they would cooperate fully to implement it. Accordingly, the additional information convinced the decision makers to adopt a program that appeared to be slightly more costly than another alternative, because the judgment was that with a full adoption it would be less problematic. The decision makers concluded that teacher enthusiasm more than compensated for the slight difference in cost, and that Program B was more likely to succeed than Program A, when fully implemented, in reducing the cost per prevented dropout.

Using Reports that Provide Cost Analyses

Presumably when studies are prepared on CB, CE, and CU analysis in education, they have implications for other settings in which similar decision problems are faced. That is, when a particular analyst devotes considerable resources to an evaluation that incorporates costs, there is certainly the possibility that the ensuing study or report will have some usefulness in other situations. This is the issue set out in Chapter 2, in which a study that is prepared for a primary audience of decision makers will also be used to inform secondary audiences. The purpose of this section is to consider the use of the results of such studies in other settings as well as the validity of such studies in such uses.

Two problems arise in considering the consequences of other studies for informing decision makers on similar problems that they face in their own settings. The first question is whether the study or report that is under consideration is an adequate analysis in terms of the standard requirements for such a work. The second is the degree to which the results of that study can be generalized to the present setting. Each of these will be considered in turn.

The reason that it is often difficult to evaluate cost-effectiveness or cost-benefit studies is that the reader of such literature normally lacks the skills to understand what issues should be raised in such a literature evaluation. Indeed, one of the underlying motives behind this presentation has been to provide enough of an understanding of these issues to provide a reader with competence to judge such studies. But the reader should bear in mind that CB and CE studies often have the status of the "emperor's new clothes," so that very poor analyses are implemented or published because there are few readers or referees that have the competence to evaluate them. While the quality of evaluation studies may be problematic in virtually all areas of educational and social evaluation, these evaluations are even more susceptible to deficiencies when cost analyses are integrated. The state of the art is simply not well advanced among evaluators, and the fact that readers will not recognize inadequacies and errors, because of their own lack of training, results in the publication of some very faulty analyses.

A second issue is the relevance of even an excellent study to a different setting. The question of generalizability from one sample or setting to another pervades the field of evaluation. Clearly, there is no simple answer to that question, but each situation requires its own analysis on how appropriate it is to apply the results of one study to a different setting. While some of the criteria that might be used to answer the question will be addressed below, it is important to note that CU analysis is so subjective that it would seem wise never to apply the CU results of one situation to another. That is, the value that is attached to alternatives is likely to be so peculiar to the specific clientele or panel of raters — and the determinants of their choices so difficult to observe or replicate — that CU analysis from one setting should not be used as a basis for making decisions in another one.

Checklist for Evaluating Cost Analysis Reports

At this point, the reader may find it useful to have a checklist of criteria for evaluating reports on cost-effectiveness analysis in education. Since the literature is most likely to provide CB and CE studies, rather than the more individualized and idiosyncratic CU studies, most of the questions relating to assessment of results refer to effectiveness. However, the questions that are pertinent to the decision framework, specification of alternatives, and costs apply to all three types of studies.

(1) *What is the decision framework?* That is, what is the specific context in which decisions must be made, and on what basis? What are the criteria that should guide the decision?

(2) *Which alternatives are evaluated?* Are these the relevant alternatives, and are there others that ought to be considered?

(3) *How are costs estimated?* Are the ingredients or resource requirements for each alternative set out carefully? Is the method for costing these ingredients appropriate? Are all of the ingredients included in the costing exercise, or does it include only those that are paid for by the sponsor?

(4) *Are the costs evaluated according to who pays them?* If relevant, is the analysis extended to a distribution of cost burdens among constituencies?

(5) *Are costs presented in an appropriate mode, given the nature of the decision context?* Is the cost analysis differentiated for different levels of scale of the alternatives? Is the appropriate cost concept used (e.g., total, average, or marginal cost) in the comparison? Are costs discounted appropriately for their distribution over the time horizon?

(6) *Is the criterion of effectiveness appropriate to the analysis?* To what degree does it omit important outcomes of the alternative that should be taken into consideration? To the degree that there are multiple outcomes, how are they taken into account? Are they weighted appropriately in ascertaining the overall effectiveness of alternatives?

(7) *Are there different distributional effects of the alternatives across populations?* Do the alternatives provide different results for different groups? For example, do some populations benefit more from one type of program while others benefit more from another type? To what degree are these differences accounted for in the analysis, and how are they considered in the evaluation of effectiveness?

(8) *Does the analysis of results meet the overall standards for assessing effectiveness?* Are the experimental or quasi-experimental design and its implementation and methodology sufficient to place high reliability on the estimated effectiveness of alternatives?

(9) *Are the cost-effectiveness comparisons appropriate?* Given all of the previous criteria, are the results used correctly to rank alternatives? What errors or omissions are evident? If these were corrected in the analysis, would the rankings change? Are the differences in cost-effectiveness values among alternatives large enough that you would have confidence in using them as a basis for decisions? How robust are they with respect to different assumptions about the ingredient requirements, imputation of costs to ingredients, choice of discount rates, measure of effectiveness, and weighing of different dimensions of effectiveness?

(10) *How generalizable are the results to other settings?* To what degree are the results likely to have wider generalizability than just the specific decision-context that is considered? For example, could they be applied to alternatives for similar populations and similar objectives in other organizational settings? Is it possible to make cost-estimate adjustments that would enable such generalizability?

Each of the items in this checklist refers to a systematic attempt to evaluate a report and to ascertain its strengths and weaknesses. The first two refer to the overall decision context in which the study is situated. The decision framework and the alternatives under scrutiny should be described explicitly in order to understand the nature of the decision problem and the alternatives that were considered in addressing it (see Chapter 2). The next three criteria refer to the procedures for estimating costs (see Chapter 3). Items 6 and 7 address the appropriate conceptualization, measures, and distribution of effects or benefits (see Chapter 4). Item 8 refers to the quality of the overall evaluation, a matter that is not extensively discussed in this work. The major issues can be found in such works on evaluation as Cook and Campbell (1979), Rossi and Freeman (1982), and Cronbach (1982). Item 9 refers to matters that were addressed at the beginning of this chapter.

The final item on generalizability essentially asks the question, To what degree was the setting for this study similar to that for other decision contexts that one might wish to apply these results? To answer that question one must look carefully at such criteria as the population, objectives, organizational issues, and all of the other factors that are similar or dissimilar between the setting in which the study took place and that for which the reader is considering applying the results. Clearly, the greater the similarities between the two, the more acceptable is some degree of generalization from one setting to the other. Caution is always wise in such an exercise, however, and one should be very wary of other factors that are not similar between the two situations and their consequences for generalizability.

Design and Implementation
of Studies – Next Steps

As stated in Chapter 1, the purpose of this primer is to familiarize the reader with the importance, utilization, conceptualization, and application of cost-analysis approaches to educational evaluations. Although the purpose was not to provide expertise in producing such studies — a goal that would be impossible to attain in the absence of substantial training and exposure to the field — it was suggested that this primer can be the first step in obtaining the background necessary to carry out such studies. In this final section a number of other steps are presented for moving in this direction.

What Expertise is Needed?

In most CB or CE evaluations some expertise will be needed from persons who are specialists in these kinds of analyses. Accordingly, it is important to suggest the kinds of expertise that might be needed. The evaluation analyst who requires assistance to develop CB or CE evaluation optimally should select a recognized expert who has done these types of evaluations before and whose work is recognized widely as being of high quality. Unfortunately, the relatively recent interest in incorporating CB or CE approaches into social evaluations has meant that there are relatively few such experts. Thus one might wish to ascertain where expertise might be obtained.

Almost any university economics department with a doctoral-level training program will have specialists in economic aspects of evaluation. Cost-benefit analysis, in particular, is a standard component in the study of public finance or government finance. That area addresses itself, in part, to efficiency in government spending and to maximizing social welfare (Musgrave & Musgrave, 1976, Chaps. 5-7; Little, 1957). For this reason, at least rudiments of cost-benefit analysis will be familiar to virtually all doctoral-level economists who have specialized in government or public finance. In addition, the tool has become increasingly prominent in graduate-level curricula in public policy and public management. Throughout the nation, universities have initiated graduate programs in these areas. While students receiving master's degrees in such programs are likely to possess only a consumer's knowledge of the CB and CE tools, some of the doctoral students will have specialized in this area of research.

In seeking expertise it is important to ascertain the relevance of the experience of the potential expert to the particular problem that will be raised. One should not assume that every public finance or public policy economist is an expert in CB or CE analysis without scrutinizing articles and reports prepared by that person. If the previous work of the prospective expert looks competent and creative and potentially applicable to the problem of interest, it is likely that the person will provide productive assistance. In part, the purpose of this chapter is to assist the evaluator in making an assessment of prospective consultants. Above all, one should not confuse expertise in accounting with expertise in CB or CE analysis. While CB and CE analysts must have a good understanding of cost accounting, cost accountants need have no understanding of CB and CE analysis. Often the correct approaches for cost accounting for business firms are inappropriate for estimating the costs of social projects. In fact, one of the dilemmas of public economics is that frequently social costs and benefits differ considerably from private ones. Cost accountants are not trained to address social costs and benefits.

Working with the Expert

One of the main purposes of this chapter has been to familiarize administrators and evaluators with the importance and requirements of cost analysis. It is hoped that this familiarity will assist them in working with the cost expert in a number of ways. First, it should assist the evaluator in finding and selecting a consultant on the CB, CE, or CU aspects of the evaluation. Second, it should enable the evaluator to work more productively with cost analysts, by providing an understanding of the basis and overall methodology of the cost-benefit and cost-effectiveness approaches. Normally, when a person is not familiar with a methodology or its terminology, he or she tends to assume that the expert has the answers. However, the premise of this chapter is that there must be an overlap in terms of knowledge among analysts in order for productive collaboration to take place.

Finally, a creative collaboration with an expert in economic evaluation requires that the overall evaluation problem be cast in a specific framework that incorporates cost-benefit or cost-effectiveness analysis appropriately. In this respect, the evaluator should be able to conceptualize the nature of the CB, CE, or CU analysis that corresponds to the particular decision problem that is posed. Although expertise may be needed on the precise measurement of costs and benefits, or effects, the actual formulation of the conceptual framework should not be the sole province of the consultant. Rather, it should be based upon an overall understanding by the administrator and evaluator of what is appropriate to the problem. The review of illustrations and concepts from this primer should be of assistance in providing a foundation of knowledge for the evaluator who lacks skills in economic analysis.

Incorporating Cost Analysis into Evaluation Designs

A final concern is the need to incorporate cost analysis into the evaluation design itself, rather than rely upon the collection of cost data as an afterthought. Clearly, once it has been determined that a CB, CU, or CE study is appropriate, the provision for collecting data on costs is just as important as the provision for data collection on effects. It is much easier to obtain accurate cost estimates when analytic procedures are built into the evaluation design than it is to later collect them on a post hoc basis, because it is possible to account more fully for the resource ingrdients that are incorporated into each alternative during the actual functioning of the evaluation. In fact, it is often impossible to ascertain the precise resources that were used after the evaluation of effectiveness has been completed.

Accordingly, an attempt should be made to construct procedures for accounting for ingredients and assessing their costs in the evaluation design itself. Such an effort will provide more accurate and systematic estimates of the costs of the alternatives, and it may also reduce the costs of data collection. (The procedures set out in Chapter 3 set out a straightforward design for collecting cost data.)

A Final Word

This primer was designed for a wide audience with differing proficiencies in evaluation and economics and with differing expectations for their use of cost analysis. However, those who wish to use the tools provided in this primer will wish to read specific studies that have applied the tools to education and other areas. For this purpose, Appendix B contains a bibliography of references that are divided according to specific applications of the methodologist in education. Other readers will wish to seek out studies that apply the tools to their substantive areas of endeavor.

Exercises

1. Assume that you undertake a cost-effectiveness study of alternative ways of improving the mathematics proficiencies of high school students in your state. Your report will be sent to school administrators in all of the school districts. What advice would you give them in considering how to apply the results of your report to their districts?

2. Why should secondary audiences be cautious about using CU results that were done for a primary audience?

3. Take a specific CE study, possibly from Appendix B. Use the checklist for evaluating cost analysis reports in order to assess that study.

4. Identify sources of local expertise in cost analysis and in evaluation design. What criteria have you used?

5. What types of assistance would you need in doing a cost evaluation, and what types of expertise could you contribute to the activity?

Appendix A

Feedback on Exercises

The purpose of this appendix is to provide feedback on the exercises. This will enable you to test your understanding of the material. The nature of the questions in the exercises varies substantially. Some of the questions call for specific answers, while others suggest a discussion of issues. Still others ask you to construct examples for analysis. In some cases there is a single answer or best answer. In others there are many alternatives, but each must be qualified on the basis of the assumptions that you are making. Finally, some answers are spelled out in great detail in the text and require only referring to those sections for review. For these reasons, it is not possible to provide in this section a concise answer to every question in the exercises, for there may not be a single answer for the open questions, and we do not wish to reproduce the lengthy discussions in the text. However, an attempt has been made to provide feedback in each case that should be of assistance in responding to each question.

Chapter 1

1. Choosing the "most effective" alternative — in the absence of cost information — could increase overall costs if the "most effective" alternative were more costly relative to the effects it produces than is some other alternative. A hypothetical illustration could show two alternatives in which the higher effectiveness of one alternative was more than offset by higher costs.

2. These studies do not meet the criteria for cost-effectiveness analysis since they do not take account of educational results. They take account only of costs and enrollments, rather than the educational effectiveness of the schools for their enrollments.

3. This information can be found in the explicit descriptions of each approach contained in the chapter.

4. (a) This situation fits a CB framework, in which one could compare the earnings of high school graduates in vocational and nonvoca-

tional curricula. For each alternative, an estimate would be made of costs and of estimated future earnings based on employment experiences and wages for recent graduates. Since the vocational curriculum is generally more costly than the others (Hu and Stromsdorfer, 1979), the benefits would have to be higher as well to justify expansion of vocational enrollments. Vocational enrollments would be expanded if the cost-benefit ratio met two criteria: It would have to be lower than that of other alternatives, and it would have to be less than 1.

A CE approach could also be used where programs were evaluated on the proportion of recent graduates who found employment within some reasonable period. The costs would be measured in the same way for both types of analyses.

(b) In general, this situation suggests a cost-utility strategy, since the results cannot be evaluated in monetary terms and the measures of effectiveness for different courses would differ. The administration can nominate groups of courses that are nonmandatory and susceptible to cuts. These can be evaluated for their enrollments, teaching effectiveness, value to students, and so on, through student, parent, and administrator ratings. These ratings can be related to costs to create CU values. Those with the highest CU ratios would be cut first until the desired reduction was reached. Costs would have to include only those that could actually be reduced over the short run. For example, tenured teachers could not be cut, although they could be reassigned to other duties.

(c) This problem could be addressed with CB analysis. The costs of the program would be the new faculty, staff, and facilities that would be required. The benefits might be viewed as the additional tuition and instructional grants that could be obtained. In this case the new program would be undertaken if costs were less than benefits and if the CB ratio were lower than for other alternatives that might also be considered.

(d) This situation suggests a CF study to ascertain what the costs of the new policy would be. This can be compared with available resources.

(e) All of these alternatives can be evaluated on the basis of their contribution to student writing. Accordingly, a common measure of effectiveness can be used for the evaluation, and a CE analysis is appropriate.

(f) This is a community college version of 4(b), above, and CU analysis would be appropriate.

(g) Since both alternatives can be evaluated on a common measure of effectiveness — mathematics competencies — CE analysis can be prescribed.

Chapter 2

1. (a) There are many potential causes of declining test scores. These include a changing student composition; changes in curriculum; changes in the test instruments; poorer educational conditions, such as rising class sizes and shorter school days; changes in the home; reduced homework assignments; and so on. Problem identification would require exploring all of these possibilities through interviews and studies of school data.

(b) The two leading possibilities for low job placements are a poor job market and a poor training program. The nature of the job market can be assessed by interviewing employers of physics majors in the regions where students usually seek employment. The reputation of the college's program in physics can also be ascertained from such interviews. At the same time, it might be possible to find out from employers how physics graduates' chances for placement might be improved. This information can delineate the specific nature of the problem and where potential interventions should be considered.

(c) A budgetary deficit can be resolved through cutting expenditures or raising revenues. Therefore, both areas should be explored to understand the nature of the problem. On the revenue side, one might explore the potential areas of income, including the possibilities of greater funds from state and federal sources, from leasing or selling unused facilities, and from private sources. On the expenditure side, there are many possibilities as well. A preliminary analysis should be made of how the problem arose and how it might be addressed, including a variety of alternatives for both increasing revenues and cutting expenditures.

(d) It is important to understand why the university is seeking to replace its mainframe computer. Is the equipment inadequate for the present or projected workload? Is it too expensive to use or maintain relative to more modern equipment? Does it lack the capabilities for meeting certain needs? All of these questions are important for setting out alternatives. For example, if it does not have the capabilities for meeting certain needs, it may be possible to meet these at minimal cost by using a computer service or time-sharing system to supplement the mainframe unit. If there is an overload, it might be useful to consider microcomputers to handle some of the simpler tasks that are presently relegated to the mainframe.

2. There are a great many possibilities. Many of these were referred to above and should be developed more fully here.

3. In each case the primary audience would be composed of those groups that have a direct stake in the decision. The secondary audience would be composed of those groups that have an interest in the evaluation for other purposes. Obviously, the specific answers will depend on your response to the previous question.

4. The answers depend on the nature of the problem and the alternatives that you have selected.

5. Once you have set out the problem and alternatives, it is possible to determine if a formal cost analysis is worthwhile by assessing what might be gained and what the evaluation might cost. The question of what might be gained by the evaluation hinges on the importance of what is at stake. If one is referring to programs with large cost implications, it is more likely that the findings can save substantial resources relative to doing no analysis. Much of this assessment will be intuitive and subjective. If it appears that the decision process will not be responsive to a cost evaluation, it may not be worth doing. The approximate cost of the evaluation can be determined by doing a rough assessment of the resources that will be required.

Chapter 3

1. The term "cost" refers to a sacrifice of some valued alternative.

2. (a) A day spent in obtaining a passport is a day lost from other endeavors, such as work or leisure. The value of what was lost might be calculated from the earnings that one could have obtained by working instead of renewing the passport.

(b) At a first glance, the cost of your failure to keep records would appear to be the additional amount of tax that had to be paid, which could have been avoided with sufficient documentation. However, we must bear in mind that there is a cost to maintaining records on the pertinent transactions. Therefore, the net cost of the situation is the difference between what would have been saved on taxes and the cost of maintaining the necessary documentation. It is possible that the cost of maintaining records would have been greater than the tax saving for doing so.

(c) The costs are determined by the resources required for the party, as well as those required to restore the lawns and shrubbery.

(d) The cost to the school of the teacher patrols is what is being given up by using teachers in that way rather than for instruction.

(e) The completion of the M.A. has both costs and benefits. Although the benefits of completing the M.A. (such as better employment opportunities or higher earnings) are sacrificed by not completing it, there are also cost savings attached to not diverting time and resources in that direction. Thus the cost can be determined only by ascertaining what benefits are being lost by deferring the M.A. and what costs are saved by that deferral. The net cost is the difference between the benefits that are lost and the costs that are saved.

3. These details are found in the text under the section on the "Inadequacy of Budgets for Cost Analysis."

4. The nature of the ingredients approach is also found in the text of this chapter.

5. (a) The ingredients include the facility, parent volunteers, tutors, materials, resources for training, and professional staff. Try to describe each of these in more detail on the basis of some hypothetical set of requirements. For example, the facility would include one regular classroom with its share of energy requirements, maintenance, furnishings, and insurance.

(b) The ingredients would include the coaches and other personnel, equipment and uniforms, space to practice, insurance, transportation requirements for travel to competitions, and so on. Try to provide more detail.

(c) The school district would need to consider such personnel as administrators, teachers, audiologists, health personnel, facilities, equipment, materials and supplies, and so on. Try to develop more details.

(d) Ingredients would include those required for the new curriculum and teacher retraining. Curriculum costs would be associated with such ingredients as new materials and equipment. Retraining costs would entail the costs of such ingredients as trainers, space for retraining, additional time commitments for teachers to permit retraining or substitute teachers to allow regular teachers to take retraining during regular school hours, and so on. Try to develop more details.

Chapter 4

1. Market prices refer to prices that are determined in the open and competitive marketplace. A definition can be found in the chapter. They should be used whenever an ingredient is purchased in such a market. Usually there is a reasonably competitive market for teachers, so teacher

salaries and fringe benefits can be viewed as the market price for a teacher with particular characteristics.

2. A shadow price refers to some value that is placed on an ingredient in the absence of a market price. It could be the equivalent of the market price if there were a market for the ingredient. Essentially, it is an attempt to use market-type principles to place a price on an ingredient where that information cannot be obtained directly from the marketplace. An example would be using the leasing cost of equivalent space as the shadow price of an educational facility that has been allotted by the school district for an intervention.

3. The use of market prices assumes that virtually an unlimited amount of a resource or ingredient could be obtained at that price. However, in many cases resources may be scarce and may have to be bid away from alternative uses to obtain more of them. In those cases any increase in demand to meet the needs for future replications may be faced with a rise in price for the ingredient. The problem is that we must make some assessment of how much the price will rise to meet the replication requirements.

4. To the degree that paid personnel are obtained in competitive markets, it is desirable to use their actual salaries and fringe benefits to determine their cost. The value of volunteers can be ascertained by determining what it would cost to obtain similarly qualified personnel to perform the same tasks.

5. The costs of facilities can be ascertained in two ways. The easiest is to take the lease or rental value of the facilities. Of course, if the facility is used for a number of activities, only that portion used for the intervention under scrutiny should be included in the cost. In the case in which the facility is not leased and no lease value can be determined, one can determine the value by knowing the replacement cost, the life of the facility, and the interest rate for this type of investment. Given that information, Table 4.1 can be used to determine the proportion of the replacement cost that is equal to the "annualized" cost of the facility.

6. At an interest rate of 5 percent the annualized value would be $71,000; at 10 percent it would be $110,200; and at 15 percent it would be $154,700.

7. About $98,850.

8. The answer is similar to that for facilities in item 5, above.

9. $2,229.

Chapter 5
1. To answer this question, construct worksheets for estimating costs for each alternative. On the basis of the description for the interventions,

suggest the ingredients that might be relevant. Follow the procedures set out in Chapter 4 for ascertaining how costs would be estimated. Remember that the cost of identifying the "potential dropouts" is common to both programs and should not be charged to either one. Alternative A will require counseling, facilities, and some clerical and record-keeping activities. Alternative B would require some placement and clerical functions. Please provide some details.

2. This question requires you to allocate the costs among the various constituencies on the worksheet and to calculate the net costs. The details are found in the text of this chapter.

3. This question assumes that the cost-effectiveness rankings will be based on the overall costs and effects from a societal perspective. However, the sponsor or other constituencies may face different costs and effects. Differences in costs may be created by both ingredients and cash subsidies from one constituency to another. Differences in effects may be created by particular constituencies valuing effects only for their members. On this basis, the cost-effectiveness ranking for a particular decision maker representing a particular constituency may differ from the overall ranking.

4. Costs are most uncertain for ingredients that are in the developmental stage (e.g., technological applications) and those for which neither market prices nor shadow prices are readily apparent. Provide specific illustrations from your own experience. The procedures for a sensitivity analysis can be found in the text of this chapter.

5. Two changes can take place in the future. The ingredients requirements can change, and the cost of the ingredients can change. For most programs we are assuming the same ingredients from year to year. If the ingredients differ over time, it is important to do a multiyear project evaluation with discounted present values among the alternatives. Changes in price levels will affect the monetary costs of ingredients and their monetary values over time. If you wish to ascertain the costs in following years, it is important to adjust for anticipated changes in prices.

6. The time pattern of resource deployment is important because resources needed in the present require greater sacrifices than those that will be required in the future. When resource use is deferred, those resources can be used for other purposes until they are needed for the intervention. Accordingly, a sum of annual costs is not adequate in itself. We must also make adjustments for the time pattern of the cost allocations by using present-value calculations for all alternatives.

7. The conceptual basis is that the present-value calculation discounts or reduces the *value* of future resource requirements relative to present ones. That is, future cost outlays of a particular amount will be weighed less heavily than equivalent outlays at present.

8. The simple summation of costs for the seven years is $124,300. Their present value at a 5 percent discount rate is about $105,400. Their present value at a 10 percent discount rate is about $90,800.

9. Cost feasibility is determined by comparing resource availability of a constituency with the costs of each alternative. Since Table 5.1 enables you to determine the costs of each alternative for each constituency, these results can be contrasted with the resource constraints for each constituency. Let us say that a CF calculation is made for a number of alternatives. For at least one of them, the cost to the sponsor exceeds the cost constraint of the sponsor. If it appeared that this alternative were particularly attractive, the sponsor might wish to solicit additional resources from other constituencies to bring the alternative within the boundaries of cost-feasibility.

10. The analysis should be based upon marginal costs and effects whenever the interventions are add-ons to existing programs. An example would be the case of alternative programs to increase reading speed, where all of the possibilities would provide additional resources while not altering the basic program.

11. The main issue involved here is that the ranking of CE alternatives for small-scale interventions might not be pertinent for large-scale ones. The larger the scale (e.g., enrollment level) of an intervention, the greater the advantages of alternatives with large fixed-cost components. The smaller the scale of an intervention, the greater the advantages of alternatives with large variable-cost components. Therefore, interventions should be evaluated for variable versus fixed costs and the implications that this will have on cost-effectiveness when shifting interventions from a single school to a school district.

Chapter 6

1. Educational interventions that prepare persons for labor markets and employment lend themselves best to CB analyses. Since a major focus of such projects is to improve employment and wages, the overall results can be viewed in terms of the additional earnings associated with the education or training.

2. The focus of the evaluation would be to compare the costs of each program with its benefits. Costs can be estimated using the ingredients basis to obtain a cost per graduate. Costs should also include the forgone earnings of the individual while undergoing training. Benefits can be assessed by doing a follow-up on recent graduates to obtain their employment experiences and wages. These can be used to construct estimates of annual

earnings per graduate. The overall benefit of each program would be the additional annual earnings per graduate relative to what would have been received without the training. Poor placements will be reflected in unemployment, which will result in low annual earnings for graduates.

CB ratios can be calculated for each program. The necessary condition for retention of a program is that the CB ratio be less than 1, so that costs are less than benefits. The sufficient condition is that the CB ratio be acceptable in that it is in the same range or lower than CB ratios for alternative programs.

3. The answer will depend upon which evaluation you choose to address.

4. The answer will depend upon which evaluation you chose in Exercise 3.

5. This is best couched as a CE problem in which the different alternatives are viewed for their effectiveness in mathematics and science instruction. That is, a common measure of effectiveness, such as a test score, can be used for each instructional domain. The alternatives can be evaluated for their effects on test scores through standard evaluation design. Each alternative should be evaluated for its ingredients requirements and costs. Costs should also be distributed among constituencies. This distribution will show, for example, that the cost to the sponsor of contributed scientists and mathematicians from industry will be low, even though the cost to industry will be high.

6. The advantages of CU in comparison with CE and CB are its flexibility in time and resource requirements; its use of a variety of existing information on the interventions, including the knowledge, experience, and intuition of the decision makers; and its ability to draw upon the judgments of stakeholders and to address several outcomes. The disadvantage is that the results are largely subjective, so that they are not replicable or generalizable from situation to situation.

7. "Utility" refers to an attempt to measure the degree of happiness or satisfaction provided by an activity. In a more applied sense it refers to the value of an activity. Utility scales are used to rate activities according to their value to the rater or to some constituency whom he or she represents. The major problems in measuring utility include (1) developing interval scales; (2) reconciling interrater comparisons of utility; (3) aggregating individual utility scales to create a measure of social utility. These points can be developed more fully in your answer.

8. A CU analysis of which additional language courses to offer would begin by ascertaining who the relevant audiences would be that have a

legitimate interest in the outcome (i.e., the stakeholders). Once these are identified, you should indicate the criteria that each might use to set priorities and how you would construct utility scales to measure their preferences. The costs of the alternatives would be measured using the ingredients method. A marginal-cost approach would be pertinent, since you are concerned with the additional costs of providing another year or two of instruction in a particular language. Thus it may be possible that for some languages there are teachers on the staff who could simply add a course in the language in place of other duties, while for other languages new teachers would have to be hired. The alternative combinations of languages and their costs should be formulated and compared in the CU evaluation.

9. The best way to do this is to have each stakeholder group do its evaluation of the utility of alternatives. This will enable CU comparisons for each constituency as well as various weightings of different groups' responses to see how sensitive the outcomes are to the varying influence given different groups in the decision.

Chapter 7

1. The most important point to stress is that generalizability of a state study to an individual situation is always problematic. You should ascertain the degree to which the state study is based upon students and schools that are representative of those of the specific district in question. A great deal of judgment must be added to the state results to see how they apply in any given situation. This should include various idiosyncratic factors that may or may not support your recommendations in a particular situation. You should try to be specific about which factors a local school district should consider in making this determination.

2. Secondary audiences should be cautious about using CU results that were done for a primary audience, because of the subjective nature of the CU methodology and results. That is, it is not possible to show how the audiences who made the utility rankings arrived at the utility scores. There is no way of knowing precisely what their assumptions were or what they took into consideration and whether the same set of conditions and considerations applies to another situation.

3. This requires a straightforward use of the checklist to evaluate a specific study.

4. The answer will vary according to your situation.

5. The answer will vary according to your situation.

Appendix B

Annotated Bibliography of Cost-Benefit and Cost-Effectiveness Studies in Education

Once you have completed this primer, you may wish to review specific studies using CB, CE, and CU approaches both to test your understanding of the subject and to see how the techniques have been applied in specific settings. The purpose of this annotated bibliography is to provide references both to general readings and to specific ones on cost analysis in education.

The specific studies that are listed are prominent ones, but they are not always exemplary in the sense of carefully following the methodology set out in this manual. Some are early studies that were prepared prior to the present state of the art. In other cases the studies are unclear on their methodologies. For example, many lack detail on the conceptual framework and procedures used to measure costs. Some also fail to make a distinction between the total costs of an intervention and their allocation among different constituencies. Nevertheless, these particular studies were chosen because of their diversity and interesting applications to pertinent educational issues. It is useful to test your skills and understanding by applying the checklist in Chapter 7 to each study. There are no CU studies represented on this list. CU studies are rarely published for external audiences for the reasons that have been mentioned.

Some of the studies refer to benefit-cost analysis (BC) rather than cost-benefit (CB). The only difference between BC and CB is the formulation of the numerator and denominator in the comparison. However, the confusion may lie in the fact that this transposition reverses the interpretation of results, so that instead of looking for the lowest CB ratios and those that are less than 1, we seek the highest BC ratios and those that exceed 1. Although this appears obvious, it is sometimes confusing to readers who are used to one or the other formulation.

Policy Aspects

Rivlin, A., *Systematic thinking about social issues*. Washington, DC: The Brookings Institution, 1971. A clearly written attempt to show how CB and CE studies are needed for better policy decisions.

Stokey, E., & Zeckhauser, R. *A primer for policy analysis*. New York: W. W. Norton, 1978. An excellent general introduction to using CB, CE, and CU as well as other analytic tools to address policy problems.

Methodological Aspects and Literature Surveys

Alkin, M. C., & Solmon, L. C. (Eds.). *The costs of evaluation*. Beverly Hills, CA: Sage Publications, 1983. Essays address the costs of evaluations and their implications.

Anderson, L. G., & Settle, R. F. *Benefit-cost analysis: A practical guide*. Lexington, MA: Lexington Books, 1977. An overview of CB analysis with a heavy emphasis on applications.

Haller, E. J. Cost analysis for educational program evaluation. In W. J. Popham (Ed.), *Evaluation in education*. Washington, DC: American Educational Research Association, 1974, Chapter 7 is a discussion of the use of cost analysis and its considerations for educational evaluations.

Levin, H. M. Cost analysis. In N. Smith (Ed.), *New techniques for evaluation*. Beverly Hills, CA: Sage Publications, 1981. Chapter 1 is a brief introduction to the tools of cost analysis and an evaluation of their application to a diverse set of case studies.

Levin, H. M. Cost-effectiveness analysis in evaluation research. In M. Guttentag & E. Struening (Eds.), *Handbook of evaluation research* (Vol. 2). Beverly Hills, CA: Sage Publications, 1975. Pages 89-122 provide a methodological overview of CE analysis as an evaluation tool.

Mishan, E. J. *Cost-benefit analysis*. New York: Praeger, 1976. This is the best comprehensive work on the subject, although it has been written primarily for economists rather than a broader audience.

Rothenberg, J. Cost-benefit analysis: a methodological exposition. In M. Guttentag and E. Struening (Eds.), *Handbook of evaluation research* (Vol. 2). Beverly Hills, CA: Sage Publications, 1975. A provocative exposure to the issues underlying CB analysis is provided on pages 55-88.

Sassone, P. G., & Schaffer, W. A. *Cost-benefit analysis: A handbook*. New York: Academic Press, 1978. A very basic exposition with both the strengths and weaknesses of oversimplification.

Thompson, M. *Benefit-cost analysis for program evaluation*. Beverly Hills, CA: Sage Publications, 1980. An introductory exposition with application to public health problems.

Weisbrod, B. Income redistribution effects and benefit-cost analysis. In S. Chase (Ed.), *Problems in public expenditures analysis*. Washington, DC:

The Brookings Institution, 1968. An excellent exposition of the distributional issues in CB analysis on pages 177-209.

Dropout Prevention

Levin, H. M. *The cost to the nation of inadequate education* (Report prepared for the Select Senate Committee on Equal Educational Opportunity). Washington, DC: U.S. Government Printing Office, 1972. Summarized in U.S. Senate, Select Committee on Equal Educational Opportunity, *Toward equal educational opportunity* (92nd Congress, 2nd Session, Report No. 92-000). Washington, DC: U.S. Government Printing Office, 1973). Chapter 13 is an attempt to determine the costs to the Nation of dropping out.

Weisbrod, B. A. Preventing high school dropouts. In R. Dorfman (Ed.), *Measuring benefits of government investments*. Washington, DC: The Brookings Institution, 1965. An early CB study of a program to prevent high school dropouts on pages 117-148.

Teacher Selection

Levin, H. M. A cost-effectiveness analysis of teacher selection. *Journal of Human Resources,* 1970, 5(1), 24-33. Applies CE to the issue of what types of teachers to select for improving student achievement.

Manpower Training Programs

Ashenfelter, O. Estimating the effect of training programs on earnings. *Review of Economics and Statistics,* 1978, 60(1), 47-57. Provides a creative statistical approach to trying to use earnings of a "control" group to estimate earnings effects of training programs.

Hammermesh, D. S. (Ed.). *Economic aspects of manpower training programs*. Lexington, MA: Lexington Books, 1971. An excellent compendium of studies and issues.

Hardin, E., & Borus, M. *The economic benefits and costs of retraining*. Lexington, MA: Lexington Books, 1971. An ovverall discussion of methodology and application to manpower training.

Ribich, T. *Education and poverty*. Washington D.C.: The Brookings Institution, 1968. Chapter 3 is a review of three manpower training evaluations that shows how differences in CB assumptions can create differences in estimated CB ratios.

Compensatory Education

Garms, W. I. A benefit-cost analysis of the Upward Bound program. *Journal of Human Resources,* 1971, 6(2), 206-220. An application to a specific program for preparing disadvantaged students for higher education.

Ribich, T. *Education and poverty* (Washington, DC: The Brookings Institution, 1968. Chapters 4 and 5 provide a creative approach to CB for preschool and compensatory education.

Vocational and Technical Education

Corrazzini, A. The decision to invest in vocational education. *Journal of Human Resources,* 1968, *3* (summer supplement), 82-100. One of the best comparisons and a sensitivity analysis of results under different assumptions.

Hu, T., Lee, M. L., & Stromsdorfer, E. W. Economic returns to vocational and comprehensive high school graduates. *Journal of Human Resources,* 1971, *6*(1), 25-50. One of the best analyses of estimating benefits of vocational education.

Hu, T., & Stromsdorfer, E. W. Cost-benefit analysis of vocational education. In T. Abramson, C. K. Tittle, and L. Cohen (Eds.), *Handbook of Vocational Education.* Beverly Hills, CA: Sage Publications, 1979. Chapter 8 provides the most comprehensive survey of CB studies in vocational education.

Educational Technology

Carnoy, M. The economic costs and returns to educational television. *Economic Development and Cultural Change,* 1975, *23,* 207-248. A good general exposition on the subject.

Carnoy, M., and Levin, H. M. Evaluation of educational media: Some issues. *Instructional Science,* 1975, *4,* 385-406. A critical evaluation of CB studies in educational technology, arguing that they tend to overstate benefits and understate costs.

Jamison, D. T., Klees, S., & Wells, S. *The costs of educational media.* Beverly Hills, CA: Sage Publications, 1978. A comprehensive survey and analysis of the costs of large-scale educational media projects.

Levin, H. M. & Woo, L. An evaluation of the costs of computer-assisted instruction. In E. House et al. (Eds.), *Evaluation studies review annual* (Vol. 7). Beverly Hills, CA: Sage Publications, 1982. Demonstrates the use of the ingredients approach to estimating the costs of computer-assisted instruction within a CF format (pp. 381-405).

Lumsden, K., & Ritchie, C. The Open University: A survey and economic analysis. *Instructional Science,* 1975, *4*(3/4), 237-292. Attempts to use CE to evaluate the British Open University.

Mayo, J., McAnany, E., & Klees, S. The Mexican Telesecundaria: A cost-effectiveness analysis. *Instructional Science,* 1975, *4*(3/4), 197-236. An evaluation of a large-scale intervention of educational television.

Education of the Handicapped

Conley, R. W. A benefit-cost analysis of the vocational rehabilitation program. *Journal of Human Resources,* 1969, *4*(2), 226-252. A good early CB study in vocational rehabilitation.

Hartman, W. T. Estimating the costs of educating handicapped children: A resource-cost model approach. *Educational Evaluation and Policy Analysis,* 1981, *3*(4), 33-47. A clear presentation of the methodology for estimating costs for special education.

Kakalik, J. S., Furry, W. S., Thomas, M. A., & Carney, W. F. *The cost of special education.* Santa Monica, CA: Rand Corporation, 1981. Uses an ingredients approach to provide the most comprehensive analysis of costs of different programs for the handicapped.

References

Allen, V. L. (Ed.). *Children as teachers: Theory and research on tutoring.* New York: Academic Press, 1976.

Arrow, K. J. *Social choice and individual values.* New York: Wiley, 1963.

Barker, R. G., & Gump, P. V. *Big school, small school – High school size and student behavior.* Stanford, CA: Stanford University Press, 1964.

Baumol, W. J. On the social rate of discount. *American Economic Review,* 1968, *58,* 788-802.

Becker, G. *Human capital.* New York: Columbia University Press, 1964.

Berman, P., & McLaughlin, M. *Federal programs supporting educational change, Vol. 4: The findings in review* (R-1589/4-HEW). Santa Monica, CA: Rand Corporation, 1975.

Byrk, A. S. (Ed.). Stakeholder-based evaluation, (special issue). *New Directions for Program Evaluation,* 1983, *17*(March).

Chambers, J. The development of a cost of education index. *Journal of Education Finance,* 1980, *5*(3), 262-281.

Chambers, J. An analysis of school size under a voucher system. *Educational Evaluation and Policy Analysis,* 1981, *3*(2), 29-40.

Cohen, D. K. Politics and research: Evaluation of social action programs. *Reviews of Educational Research,* 1970, *40*(2), 213-238.

Cohn, E. *The Economics of Education* (Rev. ed.). Cambridge, MA: Ballinger, 1979.

Cook, T. D., & Campbell, D. T. *Quasi-experimentation.* Chicago: Rand McNally, 1979.

Cronbach, L. J. *Designing evaluations of educational and social programs.* San Francisco: Jossey-Bass, 1982.

Dorfman, R. *Prices and markets.* Englewood Cliffs, NJ: Prentice-Hall, 1967).

Eckaus, R. *Estimating the returns to education: A disaggregated approach.* New York: Carnegie Commission on Higher Education, 1973.

Eckstein, O. *Water-resource development.* Cambridge, MA: Harvard University Press, 1958.

Edwards, W., & Newman, J. R. *Multiattribute evaluation.* Beverly Hills, CA: Sage Publications, 1982.

Fishburn, P. *Decision and value theory.* New York: Wiley, 1964 .

Halevy, E. *The growth of philosophic radicalism.* Boston: Beacon Press, 1955.

Hanoch, G. An economic analysis of earnings and schooling. *Journal of Human Resources,* 1967, *2*(3), 310-329.

Hu, T., & Stromsdorfer, E. W. Cost-benefit analysis of vocational education. In T. Abramson, C. K. Tittle, and L. Cohen (Eds.), *Handbook of vocational education evaluation.* Beverly Hills, CA: Sage Publications, 1979.

Jamison, D. T., Klees, S. J., & Wells, S. J. *The costs of educational media.* Beverly Hills, CA: Sage Publications, 1978.

Keeney, R., & Raiffa, H. *Decisions with multiple objectives: Preferences and value tradeoffs.* New York: Wiley, 1976.

Levin, H. M. Cost-effectiveness in evaluation research. In M. Guttentag and E. Struening (Eds.), *Handbook of evaluation research* (Vol. 2). Beverly Hills, CA: Sage Publications, 1975.

Levin, H. M. Cost analysis. In N. Smith (Ed.), *New techniques for evaluation.* Beverly Hills, CA: Sage Publications, 1981.

Little, I. M. D. *A critique of welfare economics* (2nd ed.). Oxford, England: Oxford University Press, 1957.

Mishan, E. J. *Cost-benefit analysis.* New York: Praeger, 1976.

Musgrave, R. A., & Musgrave, P. B. *Public finance in theory and practice* (2nd ed.). New York: McGraw-Hill, 1976.

Ribich, T. I. *Education and poverty.* Washington, DC: The Brookings Institution, 1968.

Rossi, P. H., & Freeman, H. E. *Evaluation: A systematic approach.* Beverly Hills: Sage Publications, 1982.

Scriven, M. Evaluation perspectives and procedures. In J. W. Popham (Ed.), *Evaluation in education: Current applications.* Berkeley, CA: McCutchan, 1974.

Stokey, E., & Zeckhauser, R. *A primer for policy analysis.* New York: W. W. Norton, 1978.

Suppes, P., & Morningstar, M. Computer-assisted instruction. *Science,* 1969, *166,* 343-350.

Weisbrod, B. A. *External benefits of public education.* Princeton, NJ: Industrial Relations Section, Princeton University, 1964.

Weisbrod, B. A. Preventing high school dropouts. In R. Dorfman (Ed.), *Measuring Benefits of Government Investments.* Washington, DC: The Brookings Institution, 1965.

Weisbrod, B. A. Income redistribution effects and benefit-cost analysis. In S. B. Chase, Jr. (Ed.), *Problems in public expenditures analysis.* (Washington, DC: The Brockings Institution, 1968.

Weiss, C. H. Evaluation research in the political context. In E. L. Struening and M. Guttentag (Eds.), *Handbook of evaluation research* (Vol. 1). Beverly Hills, CA: Sage Publications, 1975.

Index

About the Author

Henry M. Levin is a professor in both the School of Education and the Department of Economics, and director of the Institute for Research on Educational Finance and Governance, at Stanford University. He is a former fellow of the Center for Advanced Study in the Behavioral Sciences. Prior to his arrival at Stanford in 1968, he was a research associate in the Economic Studies Division of The Brookings Institution. He has also taught at Rutgers and New York Universities. Dr. Levin has advised many state and federal agencies on issues in public finance, economics of education, and cost-effectiveness analysis; he is currently a consultant to the World Bank. He has published over 100 scholarly articles and is the author or co-author of eight books. He served as president of the Evaluation Research Society in 1982.